Rightness
and Reasons

ALSO BY THE AUTHOR

Critical Essays on the Philosophy of R.G. Collingwood, ed., 1972

The Concept of Creativity in Science and Art, ed., with Denis Dutton, 1981

Relativism: Cognitive and Moral, ed., with Jack W. Meiland, 1982

Rationality, Relativism and the Human Sciences, ed., with Joseph Margolis and Richard Burian, 1986

Relativism: Interpretation and Confrontation, ed., 1989

The Interpretation of Music: Philosophical Essays, ed., 1993

Rightness and Reasons

INTERPRETATION IN CULTURAL PRACTICES

Michael Krausz

CORNELL UNIVERSITY PRESS

ITHACA AND LONDON

Copyright © 1993 by Cornell University

All rights reserved. Except for brief quotations in a review, this book, or parts thereof, must not be reproduced in any form without permission in writing from the publisher. For information, address Cornell University Press, Sage House, 512 East State Street, Ithaca, New York 14850.

First published 1993 by Cornell University Press.

International Standard Book Number 0-8014-2846-7
Library of Congress Catalog Card Number 93-12627

Printed in the United States of America

Librarians: Library of Congress cataloging information appears on the last page of the book.

∞ The paper in this book meets the minimum requirements of the American National Standard for Information Science—Permanence of Paper for Printed Library Materials, ANSI Z39.48-1984.

For Connie, without whom...

A well-schooled man is one who searches for that degree of precision in each kind of study which the nature of the subject at hand admits.
—Aristotle, *Nichomachean Ethics*

The game is won not by the player who can reconstitute what really happened, but by the player who can show that his view of what happened is the one which the evidence accessible to all players, when criticized up to the hilt, supports.
—R. G. Collingwood, *Essays in the Philosophy of History*

A fact is like a sack which won't stand up when it is empty. In order that it may stand up, one has to put into it the reason and sentiment which have caused it to exist.
—Luigi Pirandello, *Six Characters in Search of an Author*

Societies, like lives, contain their own interpretations.
—Clifford Geertz, *The Interpretation of Cultures*

Contents

List of Illustrations — ix
Acknowledgments — xi
   Introduction — 1

Part I Interpretation in Cultural Practices

1 Rightness and Reasons in Musical Intrepretation — 13

2 Cultural Practices and the Ideals of Interpretation: Singularism and Multiplism — 38

3 Imputational Interpretation in Art, Poetry, Persons, and Cultures — 66

4 Imputation and the Comparison of Interpretations — 93

Part II Interpretation without Ontology

5 Objects-of-Interpretation and Their Indeterminacy — 119

6 Historical Interpretation without Ontology — 131

7 Praxial Ideality without Ontological Realism	146
Conclusion	162
Appendix From an Interview with a Luo Medicineman	167
Index	171

Illustrations

1. Ideality and ontology 9
2. Beethoven's First Symphony, first movement, upbeat to the Allegro con brio 21
3. Singularism and multiplism 42
4. Pluralizing objects-of-interpretation 55
5. Aggregating objects-of-interpretation 57
6. Pluralizing interpretations 58
7. Aggregating interpretations 58
8. Face-vase figures 68
9. Vincent Van Gogh, *The Potato Eaters* 71
10. Lucas Samaras, *Head Transformation* 124–25

Acknowledgments

Over the years I have had many discussions with friends and colleagues about interpretation in cultural practices, and they have offered helpful and sometimes extensive suggestions about this work. I am most pleased to acknowledge Frances Berenson, Rebekah Brock, Noel Carroll, Arindam Chakrabarti, William Dray, Susan Feagin, Patrick Gardiner, Peter Hacker, Bernard Harrison, Michael Hones, Frank Hunt, Joseph Margolis, Bimal Matilal, Mary Mothersill, David Novitz, Hans Oberdiek, David Pears, Frederik Prausnitz, Laurent Stern, J. D. Trout, James Winn, and Eddy Zemach. I have also benefited from the discussions at the National Endowment for the Humanities Institute on Interpretation, University of California at Santa Cruz in 1988, and, over the years, at the conferences and workshops of the Greater Philadelphia Philosophy Consortium.

I am grateful to respective publishers for permission to rework materials of mine which have appeared in the following: "Creating and Becoming," in Denis Dutton and Michael Krausz, eds., *The Concept of Creativity in Science and Art* (The Hague: Martinus Nijhoff Publishers, 1981); "Art and Its Mythologies: A Relativist View," in Joseph Margolis, Michael Krausz, and Richard Burian, eds., *Rationality, Relativism, and the Human Sciences* (The Hague: Martinus Nijhoff Publishers, 1986); "Intentionality, Expressive Properties, and

Popper's Placement of Music," *Manuscrito* 9, no. 2 (October 1986); "Introduction," in M. Krausz, ed., *Relativism: Interpretation and Confrontation* (Notre Dame: Notre Dame University Press, 1989); "Interpretation and Its Art Objects: Two Views," *The Monist,* April 1990; "History and Its Objects," *The Monist,* April 1991; "Ideality and Ontology in the Practice of History," in W. J. Van der Dussen and L. Rubinoff, eds., *Objectivity, Method, and Point of View* (Leiden: E. J. Brill Publishers, 1991); "Intention and Interpretation: Hirsch and Margolis," in Gary Iseminger, ed., *Intention and Interpretation,* (Philadelphia: Temple University Press, 1992); "Rightness and Reasons in Musical Interpretation," in Michael Krausz, ed., *The Interpretation of Music: Philosophical Essays* (Oxford: Clarendon Press, 1993). I also thank Luo medicineman Tago Athieno for permission to include materials drawn from an interview I conducted with him in Nairobi in 1985 (see Appendix A).

Bryn Mawr College supported my work for five terms at Oxford University, 1986–90, during which time I presented some of this material in seminars co-taught with Bimal Matilal. I also thank the principals of Linacre College, John Bamborough and Sir Bryan Cartledge, and Vice-Principal Rom Harré, who facilitated my work while I was at Oxford.

I am indebted to Lorraine Kirschner for her assistance in seeing this work through its stages. For his encouragement and sustained support special thanks are due to Roger Haydon, editor of Cornell University Press.

M. K.

Rightness
and Reasons

Introduction

Which interpretation of Beethoven's First Symphony is the single right one: one that strictly adheres to the score or one that does not? Which interpretation of Van Gogh's *Potato Eaters* is the single right one: a formalist, psychological, Marxist, or feminist one? Which interpretation of Wordsworth's Lucy poem is the single right one: a pantheistic or a lifeless one? Which interpretation of life processes is the single right one: a process-centered one or a product-centered one? Which interpretation of incest is the single right one: a Judeo-Christian one or an East African Luo one? In this book I shall explore some of the assumptions of, and possible answers to, these questions.

It is perhaps natural to expect that the ideal result of an informed discussion should be the single right interpretation of a given object of inquiry. This expectation is fueled by certain examples from mathematics and physical sciences. But it is by no means clear that such a "singularism," as I shall call it, should be adopted as an ideal for the full range of human practices. In considering representative human studies—including those in which persons and cultures are taken as salient—I shall resist the singularist ideal, largely because it does violence to the nature of those cultural practices. To say this much, though, does not commit us to holding that pertinent objects have essential natures or that they constitute natural kinds. The natures of cultural entities need not be understood as historically fixed. Yet given their natures in history they may still be violated if we impose inappropriate interpretive ideals upon them. So, in considering the question whether one should characteristically seek a single right interpretation of cultural objects, I shall not assume that they are fixable independent of historically variable practices.

The singularist holds that interpreters should always pursue a single right interpretation. As we shall see, among theorists of interpretation in cultural practices singularism is well represented, although these thinkers may not identify themselves by this name. In the theory of literature, for example New Critic Monroe Beardsley, intentionalist E. D. Hirsch, and postulationist Alexander Nehamas share a commitment to singularism (whatever else divides them). In science one finds it in philosophers as diverse as Rudolf Carnap and Karl Popper. In musical performance, one finds it well represented in the so-called authentic music movement. And in theory of history one finds it in works of Patrick Nowell-Smith among others.

The multiplist denies the singularist ideal by contending that for some practices such a leading principle is misplaced, that violence would be done to the practice if such a singularism were pressed. But multiplism need not lead to interpretive anarchism. The multiplist holds that there may be reasoned critical comparison between contending interpretations. Yet such critical comparison would not show that a preferred interpretation was strong enough to unseat its rivals conclusively and render them inadmissible. So, while the singularist holds his or her preferred interpretation to be conclusively right, the multiplist may hold his or her preferred interpretation to be inconclusively so. In providing a heuristic that is an alternative to the singularist's, the multiplist exhibits an interpretive tolerance that representative cultural practices demand.

I shall argue that, while singularism may well be adopted as a regulative ideal in some cases, it should not be universally adopted as a sine qua non of rational interpretation. In this book I point to certain features of some cultural practices to show why singularism should not be universally adopted, and why multiplism may well be characteristic of the cultural practices considered.

For the reader who holds from the start that singularism is im-

INTRODUCTION 3

plausible, I offer the present book as a basis for further exploration of the multiplist program. From the reader who recognizes him or herself in my characterization of singularism, I invite counterarguments to those offered here.

My characterizations of singularism and multiplism should be taken as idealizations to help formulate, in a piecemeal way, interpretative strategies for cultural practices. My chief aim is to provide conceptual tools with which to pursue fine-grained discussions of interpretations in specific cultural practices. So understood, with the aid of representative cases, this work seeks to set out strategic moves that singularists and multiplists deploy in interpreting cultural practices. First, it is not meant as a substitute for fine-grained discussions of particular cases; rather it is intended to serve as something of a methodological contribution toward such discussions. Although its idiom is philosophical, its consequences bear on the full range of cultural practices. Second, armed with such strategies the inquirer may be better equipped to deal with the important question—not itself directly considered here—of the relation between cultural practices and noncultural practices.

Here one might ask in what ways the noncultural practices (including formal studies such as mathematics) can be contrasted with such human studies as music, art, history, and anthropology. The place of the natural sciences on this continuum—especially in light of post-Kuhnian philosophy of science—will be especially interesting. In a subsequent study one might ask whether one can distinguish the cultural from the noncultural realms on the basis that they characteristically reflect singularism or multiplism as interpretative ideals. It is to this larger question that the present book is preliminary.

I take my key examples of cultural practices as uncontentiously "cultural." They include interpretation of musical, artistic, literary, historical, and anthropological entities. And it is on the basis of these examples that one might be tempted to suggest that multiplism is representatively exemplified in cultural practices. Although I do not propound this thesis here, from the "social science" perspective one might ask whether these sorts of cases can be taken as truly representative. That is, one might urge that examples more truly representative of cultural practices might be found in more "scientific" fields such as sociology, psychology, or economics, whose examples, it might be held, are more conducive to singularist treatments. If so, the fact that multiplism might be most plausibly urged for the cases considered here would not weigh as heavily in licensing the suggestion that multiplism is representative of cultural practices, and one might indeed urge that it would be a mistake to take these kinds of cases as representative of cultural practices.

The question, Which of the cultural practices best represents cultural practices, echoes the question, Which of the natural sciences best represents the natural sciences in virtue of which one might generalize about the nature of the natural sciences as such. The heterogeneity of the natural sciences, both in subject and method, makes such a question wrongheaded, and the reasons for its wrongheadedness are transferable to the cultural realm. Cultural practices are also (and perhaps especially) heterogeneous as to subject and method. And so one cannot sustain the underlying assumption that there is essentially one kind of thing about which claims of representativeness in cultural practices should be made. This ground will need to be cleared in order to pursue the line of our subsequent inquiry. For the present, the primary target of the multiplist strategy is the universalism built into the singularist position. The target is the singularist's claim that his or her ideal is the sine qua non of rational conduct of inquiry. So, as I shall leave open the question about the relation between natural and cultural practices, I shall leave open the question about the relation between those cultural practices that presume to be scientific and those that do not.

Generally I urge in this book a piecemeal approach to questions concerning singularism or multiplism, or "praxial ideality" as I shall call it. I shall leave open the question whether the full range of objects of human experience, including middle-sized ordinary objects like sticks and stones, mathematical objects, and objects of physical science, is subsumable under the rubric of cultural practices. I shall leave open the question whether the natural sciences themselves are best understood as cultural practices. So I shall leave open the question whether the "physical sciences" and the "human sciences" designate an essential difference in natural kind.

The global theorist who holds that there is no difference in kind between the natural and the cultural faces the vexing double question as to which construal of what sorts of entities should be embraced as paradigmatic for his or her general program. For example, "ontological realists," as I shall call them—who hold that (among other sorts of things) ordinary middle-sized objects like sticks and stones are autonomous and independent of interpretive practices, and who offer their construal of such entities as paradigmatic for a global ontology—may encounter unease when applying their view to ever more culturally embodied entities such as works of music, art, literature, history, or cultures. At the same time, "ontological constructionists," as I shall call them—who take culturally embodied entities as fully interpreted and who take these as paradigmatic for a global ontology—may encounter corresponding unease when applying their view to ever less culturally embodied middle-sized objects such as sticks and stones. Indeed, the continuum from middle-sized objects to highly enculturated entities may or may not be smooth, and in cultural practices there may or may not be an analogue to middle-sized objects such as sticks and stones. In any event, the account of such a continuum should follow rather than precede a piecemeal consideration of pertinent sorts of cases.

It is instructive to note the opposing views of Thomas Kuhn and Charles Taylor regarding the cultural status of natural science. Kuhn, for example, holds that insofar as Aristotle and Newton conceived of their worlds differently, and insofar as there is no neutral lexicon that can fully translate the terms of one into the language of the other, they lived in different worlds. Correspondingly, their theories could not address themselves to the same "objects-of-interpretation," as I shall call them. Insofar as there is no translating between the lexicons in which Aristotle's and Newton's objects-of-interpretation are cast, there can be no real competition between them. Thus, no realism that assumes an autonomous order independent of interpretive practices as such can be usefully deployed in the natural sciences. Kuhn's view of the natural sciences has become something of a benchmark for theorists of cultural practices who see their disciplines in historicist or constructionist terms, and who have resisted a positivistic model of the natural sciences as the model for rational inquiry per se. They see the natural sciences as disciplines allied rather than as opposed to the human sciences and perhaps themselves capable of learning from the self-consciously interpretive stance of the latter. It is therefore ironic that Charles Taylor redraws the pre-Kuhnian distinction between the natural and human sciences, though clearly not in positivistic terms. He holds, for example, that although the Japanese bargain differently from the way Westerners do, all peoples live under the same heavens. Causality is in nature, and it is not a matter of consensus. The difference between the natural and human sciences, in Taylor's view, hangs on the fact that objects-of-interpretation in the human sciences, but not in the natural sciences, are self-interpreted and self-constituted. Interpretation in the human sciences is "imputational," as I shall say, whereas it is not imputational in the natural sciences. But I shall not here enter into this dispute. In this book I shall concentrate on uncontentiously cultural practices.

Generally I shall resist a foundationalism that holds that we can have access to a cultural world whose facts are independent of "praxial" activity or independent of construction in the context of practices. As a matter of history, the development of a given practice may be such that it holds out singly or multiply right interpretations as an appropriate leading principle, without grounding that ideal in a foundationalist way.

Part I will address "praxial" questions. These questions concern the analysis of the range of ideally admissible interpretations, how they relate to their objects-of-interpretation, and how interpretations may be rationally compared. I will avoid discussion about the ontology of the entities interpreted. Such avoidance is of argumentative significance, for a singularist might argue that one way to ensure his or her program is to tie the idea of a single right interpretation to the determinate autonomous object it is meant to capture. Put otherwise, one might hold that ontological realism necessitates singularism. But I shall argue that such an inference is invalid. In Part II, I shall discuss ontological realism and ontological constructionism, and I shall argue that questions of the ontology of cultural objects-of-interpretation are logically detachable from the questions of praxial ideality considered in Part I. Here I use "ontology" to range over ontological realism and ontological constructionism only. These terms pertain to the nature of entities which might be thought to lie behind or to be independent of their construction within a pertinent practice. My discussion of "ontological realism" restricts itself to those sorts of realisms that affirm that there are such entities, and as such encompasses such diverse views as naive realism and Platonism, among others. So arguments that bear on the detachability of ontology from ideality should not be taken as automatically applying to some of the many realisms that are in currency in the contemporary philosophical literature.

Correspondingly, I shall adopt an agnostic attitude with respect to whether there are practice-independent objects (be they middle-sized objects or idealized Platonic entities) and, contrary to certain realists or Platonists, I shall argue that pertinent "ontological" issues are logically detachable from the praxial considerations central to the debate between the singularist and multiplist positions. The argument for such agnosticism will mainly preoccupy us in Part II, but we may anticipate its key concerns. Rather in the spirit of a thought experiment, I shall invite the reader to consider the thesis of ontological indeterminacy. That is, if one were to theorize that practice-independent objects were capable of ensuring that the range of ideally admissible interpretations could be narrowed to a limit of one—in virtue of epistemic access to practice-independent objects and the determinacy of such objects—then one might have the beginnings of an ontological argument for praxial ideality. But I shall argue that (in addition to epistemic problems) if there is no reason to assume that ordinary middle-sized objects characteristically are determinate, and on that account practice-independent objects are incapable of reducing multiple interpretations to a limit of one, any temptation that a singularist might have to eliminate multiplist cases by grounding the discussion of praxial ideality in the ontology of middle-sized objects would be foiled. In this way, the temptation to ground praxial ideality in the ontology of pertinent entities will be found to arise from unwarranted assumptions about their determinacy. And, if this argument holds in the case of middle-sized objects, we may assume that an analogous argument will hold in the case of cultural entities. Again, this treatment will be offered in the spirit of a thought experiment, for I shall not positively theorize about the nature of middle-sized objects as such.

The treatment of praxial ideality in Part I assumes the detachability of ontology from praxial ideality, for which arguments are provided in Part II. Readers who wish first to satisfy themselves about such detachability may begin with Part II. But it would be best to consider Part I first, since many of the salient examples in cultural practices are introduced and discussed there.

In Chapter 1, I introduce the ideas of a range of ideally admissible interpretations, singularism and multiplism, and I exemplify them in the case of the interpretation of music. In Chapter 2, I treat the general characterization of singularism, multiplism, and their respective strategies in more formal terms. In Chapter 3, I contrast imputational and nonimputational sorts of interpretation, and I offer examples in art, poetry, persons, and cultures. As we shall see, imputational interpretation involves constituting features of the object-of-interpretation in virtue of interpretation as such, and this interpretation has significant bearing on the very identity of the cultural entities that would answer to singularist and multiplist conditions. In Chapter 4, I rehearse the nonimputationalist response to the imputationalist, and explicate the idea of inconclusivity (or justifying reasons without overarching standards), which is an essential ingredient of the multiplist condition. Since I am attempting to locate the singularist/multiplist controversy at the level of practice as opposed to the level of ontology, what interpretations are about is construed in an ontologically neutral way. Correspondingly, since "objects" might suggest a question-begging realistic construal at the outset, I adopt the phrase "objects-of-interpretation" to designate what interpretations are about. In Part II, Chapter 5 takes up the characterization of objects-of-interpretation and their determinancy in light of the discussion of imputational interpretation. Chapter 6, in turn, addresses the issue of the detachability of ideality (singularism versus multiplism) from ontology (ontological realism versus ontological constructionism). My argument for the detachability of ideality from ontology depends on my view that one may be a singularist and either a realist or a constructionist, and one may be a multiplist and either a realist or a constructionist. This issue is pursued in the case of the construal of historical events. Finally, in Chapter 7, I show how attempts to ground objects-of-interpretation in determinate practice-independent objects are foiled.

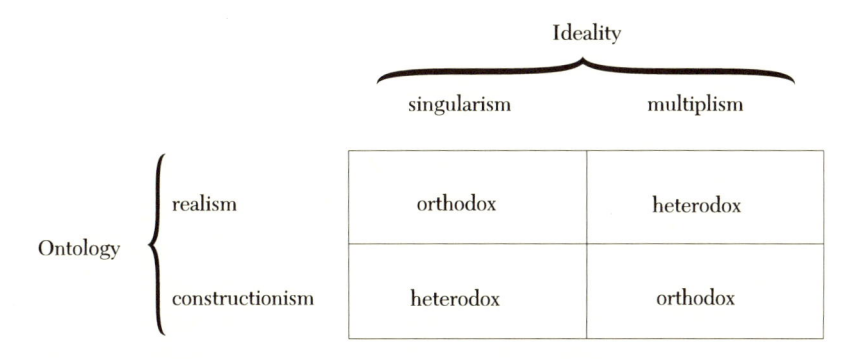

		Ideality	
		singularism	multiplism
Ontology	realism	orthodox	heterodox
	constructionism	heterodox	orthodox

Illustration 1

This argument contributes to our demonstration that ideality is logically detachable from the ontology of objects-of-interpretation. Illustration 1 may help to keep the overlapping issues in focus.

To recapitulate, the two overriding theses developed in this book may be stated straightforwardly: In pertinent cultural practices, the range of ideally admissible interpretations is characteristically multiplist rather than singularist. And praxial ideality is logically detachable from the ontology of cultural objects-of-interpretation.

Part I

INTERPRETATION IN CULTURAL PRACTICES

I

Rightness and Reasons in Musical Interpretation

As a prelude to a systematic treatment of singularism and multiplism in human practices, let us first consider the case of the interpretation of musical scores as classically construed.

No cultural entity can be understood as such independently of the practices in which it is found and fostered. Such practices provide the terms in which cultural entities can be made intelligible and appreciated. We may see this contextualism in identifying cultural entities when observing that, in order to formulate such cultural categories as music and art, for example, we need to fix upon good cases; and good cases depend on considerations of culturally and historically variable practices.

Scores in the Contexts of Practices

Consider, then, the contextuality of musical performances based on written scores. A musical score is a notation for performance, but it is characteristically incomplete in that it does not fully specify all pertinent aspects of performance. I take this incompleteness to be a feature of the entrenched genre of performance.

One might argue that this incompleteness is a contingent matter, that given sufficient subtlety of notation and completeness of description one could, in principle, specify all pertinent aspects of an admissible performance. Just as one could, in principle, provide a complete physical description of the molecules of pigment on a canvas, the argument might go, so one could give a complete physical description of the sound patterns and frequencies of a performance in a fully specified chamber. This description would presumably include all physical aspects of the sound-producing instruments as well as all aspects of the sound-producing persons, and so on. Then, according to the proposal, if one took this complete description as a set of instructions for a future performance, one would have a "complete" score. This complete score would mandate what the single ideally admissible performance should contain.

Now, on the "complete" score construal, all in-principle specifiable aspects of the performance would be defining of the work. So, for any two performances, at least one performance could not be of the given work of music, if there were any discrepancies between them. And further, since not all fully specified aspects of the completed score could even be reproduced, we could never have two performances of the same work. Given this "complete" score construal, David Oistrakh's and Nathan Milstein's performances of Bach's Partita No. 1, say, could not be both of the same work; nor could either Oistrakh's or Milstein's performances on two different occasions be of the same work.

Or consider Bryan Magee's remarks about performances of Brahms's symphonies by conductors Arturo Toscanini and Bruno Walter.

> Under Toscanini they are played with almost demonic ferocity and drive, and are deeply disturbing. Under Walter they have a glowing, autumnal relaxation and warmth, and are deeply consoling. Neither conductor transgresses the letter of the scores, nor their spirit. Yet the sum of what they bring out in them could not possibly be combined in a single performance. The acidity and cutting edge of the one entirely precludes the loving embrace of the other. High tension and heartsease are mutually exclusive. Everything each gives us is unquestionably there in the music, but for every element that is realized in performance some other has had to be sacrificed.[1]

1. Bryan Magee, *Aspects of Wagner* (London: Granada, 1968), p. 89.

Further, a range of performance practices is not fully notable in a typical score. For example, on string instruments, a multiplicity of performance practices may arise in the face of unspecified bowings, fingerings, positionings, phrasings, or the like. While fingerings and bowings may be indicated, precise finger locations and precise stresses within slurs cannot be. While positions may be indicated, the manner of sliding into and out of particular positions cannot be indicated precisely. While broad indications of vibrato speed may be given, precise indications cannot be notated. While pitch may be precisely indicated for keyboard instruments, it cannot be precisely indicated for string instruments; for example, on the latter C sharp is played slightly higher than D flat, but how much higher cannot be notated. Precise notatability fails as well for balance and pacing. Pauses and fermatas admit of significant variation. Accents and stresses may be indicated only broadly, without full precision. There is no precise volume for "forte" or "piano." And tempo is not the simple beating of time but the phenomenal experience of time. A buoyant performance whose elements are distinct and crisp will seem faster than one whose elements are less distinct and crisp—even if the latter takes the same or less clock time than the former. As conductor Riccardo Muti has said, "Tempo is not a number."[2] Toscanini's timed performances of Wagner actually took longer than expected. Yet Toscanini was famous for his faster tempi. The point is graphically illustrated by Bryan Magee:

> At Bayreuth, where they have complete recordings, the slowest *Parsifal* to date was conducted in 1931 by Toscanini (usually thought of as a fast conductor) and lasted 5 hours and 5 minutes excluding intervals. The quickest was conducted by Clemens Krauss in 1953 and lasted 3 hours and 56 minutes.... Often the figures show the facts to be contrary to a conductor's reputation—Toscanini's *Tristan*, like his *Parsifal*, was the slowest ever. Often they show that the impression of a performance which has been formed by the listener is illusory—when I heard the broadcast of Karajan's *Tristan* from Bayreuth in 1952 I thought it was one of the slowest

---

2. Riccardo Muti in conversation with the author, March 1987, and in an interview conducted by the author at the American Society for Aesthetics–Eastern Division, Philadelphia, April 21, 1989.

pieces of great conducting I had ever heard, but the figures show him to have taken it faster than all but two other conductors before or since. Beecham was also thought of as a conductor who sent things along at a pretty fast lick, but a comparison of the stopwatch timings of his performances with those of other conductors shows this not to be literally so. The impression was made by an uncommon buoyancy and spring at speeds which were fairly average. When he conducted *The Mastersingers* [sic] at Covent Garden for the first time in 1913 he was criticized for taking it so much faster than Richter (who had not just studied the work with Wagner but lived with him during its composition and helped him copy out the score) whereupon he produced timings to prove that his performance in fact took *longer* than Richter's.[3]

And even a composer may be mistaken about his assessment of the relation between clock-time and experienced performance time of his own work. Magee quotes Wagner who tells us that he furnished his early scores with what he called

> positively eloquent indications of tempo, fixing these with unmistakable precision (so I thought) by means of the metronome. But then whenever I heard about some foolishly wrong tempo in, say, a performance of my *Tannhauser,* any complaint from me was almost always met with the defense that my metronome markings had been most scrupulously observed. From this I realized how uncertain the relationship of mathematics to music must be, and not only dispensed with the metronome forthwith but contented myself with only the most general indications of even the main tempo.[4]

A typical score may comply with a range of performance practices. For example, when executing a three-note figure, violinists who favor the Paganini Stroke play one downbow and two upbows. When executing a four-note figure, those who favor the Viotti Stroke play two downbows and two upbows, and so on. These strokes are by no means mandated by most scores, and appropriate passages may be admissibly performed otherwise.

3. See Magee, *Aspects of Wagner,* pp. 92–94.
4. Ibid., p. 94.

These examples suggest that the procedures of musical practice resist rulelike formulation. Yet they can be learned through apprenticeship and experience. Indeed, much of what violin pedagogue Josef Gingold teaches master students concerns just the sorts of features mentioned above. At another level, he instills musical attitudes or approaches characteristic of a distinct performance practice. For example, he exhorts students to "live with" a musical phrase; to relent to "what the music demands"; to "make something of" the music; to "stress the unobvious"; to shape a performance that is mindful of the structure of the work, and not to be taken in "by the beauty of the sound"; to "avoid doing too much"; to "cry at every shift of position"; to play "in a modulated rather than mechanical way"; to play "with taste"; and to "keep it in."[5]

Perhaps the complete score construal is appropriate in computer music performance, where the computer program is the score and the performance is what the computer audibly produces as a mechanical function of the program. Of course, the program requires a richer (perhaps digital) system of notation than is normal for scores. Yet even here, it might be urged, the score is incomplete, for the music will sound quite different in different rooms, depending on whether they are empty or full of people or furniture and whether the sound-making devices are affected by humidity, elevation, or the like. But this variation appears to be no obstacle in principle since the richer notation might be capable of accommodating such conditions as well. Such a development would, however, constitute a shift in the very idea of a performance as classically construed. And if such a completeness were to be made a requirement for scores, they would cease to be scores in the classical sense. As distinct genres, classical performances and scores would have been violated.

Now, if we do not accept the idea of a complete score for a performance as classically construed, we must allow that there is a certain latitude between a characteristically incomplete score and an admissible performance of it. Although a score underdetermines an admissible performance of a work, a score indicates the work's "essen-

---

5. Josef Gingold in a master class at the Curtis Institute of Music, November 7, 1986, and in violin lessons with the author in years past.

tialities." And a performance must—within limits—embody those essentialities if it is to be a performance of the given work.

Performances and Interpretations

In this discussion I shall be using "interpretation" in music more or less synonymously with "performance," although for certain purposes we may note some differences between them.[6] Yet these differences will not bear on the general argument here developed. One might be tempted to speak of interpretation as bearing upon one's conception of a performance as opposed to an actual performance. It may, for example, bear on what an interpreter takes to be more or less worthy of emphasis and the like.

Different performances may be given of a particular interpretation. In general, scores underdetermine interpretations and interpretations underdetermine performances. Interpretations are more complete than scores, and performances are more complete than interpretations.[7] So, the difference between, say, David Oistrakh's and Nathan Milstein's interpretations of Bach's Partita No. 1 concerns their conceptions of the work and does not depend upon their actual performances of it. Further, either may perform his interpretation more than once. Whatever idiosyncrasies there might be between different actual performances, if conceptions of the work are appreciably unchanged, musicians may perform the same interpretation on different occasions. Put still otherwise, numerous performances may embody a single interpretation.

---

6. Following Jerrold Levinson, I shall assume the distinction between performance-interpretations and critical-interpretations, the latter—with which critics are characteristically concerned—being philosophically distinct from the former. See Levinson's "Performative vs. Critical Interpretations in Music," in Michael Krausz, ed., *The Interpretation of Music: Philosophical Essays* (Oxford: Clarendon Press, 1993).

7. I have in mind typical cases of Western notated music. The point is complicated in jazz improvisation. It is also complicated where a composer intentionally specifies instructions which cannot be performed, or where a faithful performance cannot be heard. For example, the second movement of Charles Ives's Symphony No. 4 contains scored tunes which, given other simultaneous elements, cannot be heard in a performance. And, in his "In the Alley—No. 53" (part of his "114 Songs") Ives instructs the pianist to turn the page of a newspaper with the right hand while playing the piano. This instruction appears to have nothing to do with how the hearer should hear the piece. I am indebted to Jon Newsom for these examples.

At the same time, there may be a symbiotic relation between an interpretation and an actual performance. For example, the timbre of an instrument's actual sound may well bear on the interpretation of the work, as for example, in the somber slow movement of Beethoven's Eroica Symphony. How the woodwinds' otherwise bright sound is to be muted is a matter of interpretation. The practice of seating the cellos, or sometimes the violas, to the right of the conductor, is also a performance practice. But such decisions may bear on the interpretation practice insofar as they reflect certain judgments of salience about the musical line.

The timbre or volume of an instrument's actual tone may bear upon the interpretation of the work, and vice versa. The actual instruments used or the hall in which they are played may prompt adjustments that bear directly upon one's interpretation. This is especially true of ensemble playing where adjustments to the performance inevitably give rise to adjustments of the interpretation. For example, on April 27, 1986, the Philadelphia Chamber Orchestra performed Mozart's Sinfonia Concertante in E Flat Major under guest conductor Lawrence Leighton-Smith. In rehearsal with violin soloist David Arben and viola soloist Michael Tree, it became apparent that the unforced volume of Tree's viola was too great in relation to the unforced volume of Arben's violin. The solution to this balance problem was found in physically repositioning Tree so that the F-holes of his instrument were turned further away from the audience. Exactly where he was repositioned was a matter of judgment concerning the interpretation of the work. It might appear that this is a case in which the interpretation affects the performance. So it is, to a large but limited degree, for the precise level of volume finally established as acceptable was as much a function of the unforced volume of the instruments as of interpretive considerations. In this way, interpretation practice may be symbiotically related to performance practice. But, to reiterate, this distinction between interpretation and performance will not bear directly upon the major line of the argument advanced in this book.[8] Let us return, then, to the question of the relation between scores and interpretations.

8. Indeed, if we invoke the distinction between interpretations and performances, we may say that one may be a multiplist with respect to interpretations because of the multiplicity of interpretation practices. This leaves open the possibility that for a given inter-

Admissible and Inadmissible Musical Interpretations

Now the distinction between admissible and inadmissible interpretations may be gradual rather than sharp, since certain indications that a score mandates may arguably be overridden for good reasons and the strength of those reasons may well vary. For example, one might be tempted to say that the principle of faithfulness to the score constitutes a sharp criterion for admissible interpretations. But sometimes such a criterion is contestable. A score may, for good reasons, be overridden and the resulting interpretation might still be admissible. Indeed some interpretation practices actually challenge the view that all specified features of a characteristically incomplete score should be respected. They oppose the view that all "essentialities" specified by the score are necessary for an admissible interpretation or are necessary for the identification of the work. I should hasten to add, though, that such a concession does not amount to embracing the view that all admissible interpretations are equally preferable.

For example, according to a literalist reading of waltzes, each beat in the three-beat figure is to be equally spaced. But, according to the so-called Viennese style, the second beat should be played slightly before its notated time, thus leaving an extra gap between the second and third beats. It is noteworthy that composer Johann Strauss performed his own waltzes in the Viennese style, having himself written them without special indication to do so.

Consider another case of competing interpretation practices. One calls for violating the score, and it is almost always favored for good reasons. The opposing practice calls for not violating the score, and it is favored by only a few interpreters, also for good reasons.

The first movement of Beethoven's First Symphony opens with an introductory Adagio molto of twelve bars. There follows the Allegro con brio, which constitutes the rest of the movement. Now, the upbeat to the Allegro con brio—printed still in the Adagio tempo—is almost

---

pretation there may well be one ideally admissible performance of it. That is, it may be conceded that there may be a multiplicity of interpretations and that is a separate matter from whether there might be only one ideally admissible performance of it. I am indebted to Mary Mothersill for this point.

MUSICAL INTERPRETATION

Illustration 2

always interpreted in the Allegro tempo, as if the upbeat were already in the Allegro, though according to the score it is not. The reason characteristically offered for this practice is that the upbeat—a descending scale from G to C—is repeated often within the ensuing Allegro section. Were one to interpret the work as scored, the first appearance of this figure would be anomalous; it would be taken much slower than its many repetitions in the remainder of the movement. It would violate aesthetic consistency.

Now, no one suggests that Beethoven did not mean to notate the score as he did, or that there has been an editorial error in standard editions of the score. Sergiu Comissiona and Christopher Hogwood are among only a few conductors who actually interpret the upbeat to the Allegro as literally scored. Most interpreters hold the view expressed by Riccardo Muti that it is a "mistake" to perform the work as scored.[9]

Good reasons have been given for performing the passage either way: according to the principle of faithfulness to the score, or according to the principle of aesthetic consistency. Despite the fact that the overwhelming tendency is to favor the principle of aesthetic consistency, neither is *conclusively* right. Even if Muti is correct to say that it is a "mistake" to perform the upbeat as scored because doing so violates aesthetic consistency, it cannot be *simply* wrong to do so.

9. Muti, conversation and interview.

And, to make the principle of faithfulness to the score subservient to the principle of aesthetic consistency, or vice versa, would require some overarching standard to effect such conclusive ranking. But none is available. Consequently, affirming one interpretation as ideally admissible does not exclude the other as ideally admissible. This amounts to a case of multiplism.

The difference between what is interpreted and what is notated is "the-score-in-the-context-of-interpretation-practices." Here extra-score considerations enter which are required for an adequate interpretation. In this way, as an entrenched classical genre, scores as such are in the relevant sense incomplete.

So, although what is specified in a score may be sufficient (but perhaps not fully necessary) for the identification of a work, it is not sufficient for an ideally admissible interpretation of it. Extra-score practices are required for completing the interpretation. Since these practices may vary, and no one of them can be established as the single right one, the view that there is a single right musical interpretation must yield to the view that there may be a multiplicity of ideally admissible interpretations. Where there are no univocal and overarching standards in virtue of which one may say that one among a number of interpretation practices is conclusively better than another, there can be no single ideal musical interpretation. To insist that the range of ideally admissible musical interpretations is singular is to violate an entrenched feature of classical interpretation, namely the incompleteness of scores in relation to their interpretations. So, it is a mistake to assume that there must be a single ideally admissible musical interpretation.

Counters to Multiplism in Music

If interpretation practices vary as they do, scores as classically construed must admit of a multiplicity of ideally admissible interpretations. Let us now consider some possible counters to this suggestion. A singularist might well concede that scores underdetermine interpretations. But he or she might insist that it does not follow from this that there is a multiplicity of ideally admissible interpretations. That is, such a concession does not rule out the possibility that, with sufficiently full description of the intentional context of the composer and with a sufficiently full accounting of interpretation practices and perhaps more, it will become clear that finally there can be only one ideal interpretation. A sufficiently full accounting of the score-in-the-context-of-interpretation-practices-and-more will show that, for any case, the range of ideally admissible musical interpretations is singular.

For example, one might urge that the single right interpretation is always to be found in the intentions of the composer. But this suggestion is problematic. A composer may be self deceived in regards to his or her own work. For example, Alberto Ginastera's "Concerto per Corde," contains a lengthy and exceedingly complicated solo passage of some two full pages for the concertmaster. On his own account, given pressures of rehearsal time while on tour, former Philadelphia Orchestra Concertmaster Anshel Brusilow virtually improvised the passage with only the remotest relationship to the scored pages.[10] By coincidence, Ginastera was present at the performance in Mexico City. After the concert, Ginastera eagerly sought out Brusilow to embrace him and to exclaim with delight, "I never imagined that my work could sound like *that!*"

Further, works are emergent in the sense that their finished character often embodies properties that are unanticipated. A work may embody features that the creator never intended. This means that, at least with respect to pertinent emergent properties, the creator carries no special status as one to assign salience or significance or meaning. So, contrary to proponents of the so-called authentic music movement, the intentions of a given composer need not locate or exhaust ideally admissible interpretations of a work. For these sorts of reasons, the original intentions of a creator need not fulfill the singularist's requirement.

From these remarks we may conclude that the authentic music movement cannot deliver its promise for singularly correct interpretations. However recontextualized its various devices may be, there is no way in which the original, if itself singular, can be retrieved. As Martin Donougho says: "Music never *was* 'as it actually was.' ...

---

10. Anshel Brusilow, in conversation with the author, April 12, 1987, shared here with his consent.

Scraping away the Romantic patina is one thing: actually recovering a supposed original is another."[11]

In light of these sorts of considerations, a singularist might propose that one should then *postulate* a composer—perhaps not to coincide with the historical composer—in relation to which ideally admissible interpretations should be determined.[12] The postulated composer would be an idealized creator (perhaps even a supernatural creator deity) whose (contrary-to-fact) "gaze" would be constructed based upon the work as received in the context of appropriately designated interpretive practices. He or she would be a rational reconstruction of a creator whose postulated intentions could conclusively adjudicate between competing interpretations. But consider what would be involved in postulating such a composer. What one might take as salient or significant from the background information on the basis of which to postulate a composer (that is, the work and its surrounding interpretive practices, and so forth) is already multiply interpretable. Such background information is characteristically such that no one composer can be plausibly postulated.

In response, a singularist might suggest that we should imagine a conversation with a postulated composer in which we engage him or her about a contested interpretation. We might ask a postulated Beethoven, for example, whether Muti's interpretation of the passage considered in Illustration 2 is admissible or not, whether Muti's interpretation *and* Comissiona's interpretations are both admissible, or, if they are both admissible, whether they are equally preferable. The singularist might thereby suggest that we could be justified in overriding the score only on the condition that a postulated Beethoven could be convinced that the alteration was an improvement, given Beethoven's overall intentions. That is, the changes would be justifiable on the condition that a Beethoven who reflected upon the options would have endorsed them. Without such an imprimatur the proposed interpretation could no longer present itself as an interpretation of *Beethoven's* symphony.[13]

---

11. Martin Donougho, "Music and History," in Philip Alperson, ed., *What Is Music?* (New York: Haven, 1987), p. 345.

12. See Alexander Nehamas, "The Postulated Author: Critical Monism as a Regulative Ideal," *Critical Inquiry* 8 (Autumn 1981), 133–49.

13. I am indebted to Jerrold Levinson for helpful suggestions along these lines.

Notice that the singularist who advances the postulated composer concedes that the historical Beethoven is impotent to settle the matter. But it is unclear why the exercise of postulating composer(s) should not issue in more than one postulated Beethoven (or, for the supernaturalist, more than one deity). And, to capture the point about Beethoven's imprimatur, it is unclear why any number of plausible postulations should not be put in Beethoven's name. Should we not say, rather, that given what we do know about the historical Beethoven—limited as that information must be—*we,* as unhurried interpreters think it better to interpret the work this way rather than that? Ours is a present postulation, and other postulations may be plausibly offered at other times under perhaps different circumstances. Those postulations may take different, perhaps incongruent, forms. Since a number of interpretations may be issued on the basis of a number of reasonably postulated Beethovens, it will not help to identify one single interpretation as the single admissible Beethoven interpretation.

This multiplist counterargument does not mean that all changes that produce aesthetic improvements should be the basis for admissible interpretation. While one might be tempted to "improve" upon a score, if such improvement is not in the name of the composer at all—that is, if no reasonable story can be told in which the postulation takes any account of the composer's overall project (in contrast with his or her individual intentions) it is indeed no longer an improvement on the pertinent score. The rational reconstructability of the composer's overall project will be the basis for more general conditions that constrain the range of ideally admissible interpretations. I shall return to this issue in Chapter 2. For now we may conclude that disallowing the historical composer as the final arbiter of ideal admissibility, and recognizing that the postulated composer may be multiple, does not accede to the view that any postulation or interpretation will do.

A singularist might rejoin by taking a rather different tack. He or she may concede that scores underdetermine interpretations. But it does not follow from this that there can be no single ideal interpretation. For such a concession does not rule out the possibility that with a sufficiently full accounting of competing interpretive practices—*and with something more*—it will become clear that finally there can be only one ideally admissible interpretation. That is, a sufficiently full accounting of the score-in-the-context-of-interpretive-practice-*and-more* will show that the range of ideally admissible interpretations is singular. Put otherwise, conceding the multiplicity of interpretive practices, one might appeal to yet further conditions to ensure that there always is a single right interpretation. Such an argument might proceed along the lines suggested by the pianist and music theorist Charles Rosen, although he himself does not embrace it.[14] According to this view, the single ideal interpretation is to be found above and beyond composers' intentions and interpretive practices. It is to be *found* via faithfulness to the score in conjunction with informed interpretive practices, and something that is quite illusive but altogether critical, namely a sense of rightness in execution. On this view, the single ideal interpretation is an emergent product of the score, of reconstructable composer's intentions, of interpretive practices, of a musical sense or the like, each adjusted in light of the other as the interpretation emerges. One "finds" the right interpretation by adjusting such considerations taken jointly.

But here one must question on what basis one can adjust such considerations in a singularly right way. Although an interpretation might seem to the interpreter to be necessitated, *weighing pertinent considerations as he or she does,* there seems no reason why one could not plausibly weigh those considerations differently, so that they would in turn issue in another interpretation that would as well have the appearance of necessity. Under these conditions it would still seem that more than one interpretation could appear to be "necessitated." There is nothing in this view that mandates the existence of a single overarching standard in virtue of which a multiplicity of interpretations is ruled out.

We may conclude, therefore, that in the absence of an overarching standard in virtue of which contending interpretations may be conclusively adjudicated, musical scores characteristically admit of a multiplicity of ideally admissible interpretations. One who requires that there must be a single right interpretation of musical scores as classically construed will do violence to musical interpretive practice.

14. This view is reconstructed on the basis of numerous exchanges with Charles Rosen in May 1988. Rosen himself does not embrace this view, however. See his book review "The Shock of the New," *New York Review of Books,* July 19, 1990, pp. 46, 48.

Ramifying the Multiplist Program

Let us now restate the general ideals of the singularist and the multiplist, and then ramify the multiplist's program in light of the foregoing discussion. The singularist holds that the range of ideally admissible interpretations should be singular, that the range of contending interpretations should be conclusively narrowed to a limit of one. He or she construes rightness in an exclusivist way, and takes the rightness of a given interpretation to be logically incompatible with the rightness of alternative interpretations. He or she requires that the single right interpretation should conclusively unseat alternative interpretations. The singularist holds that this condition is inherently more rational in that the most satisfactory result of informed considerations about competing interpretations is one in which there is full convergence to a single interpretation according to a single self-congruent standard. Even if, for a particular discussion, there seems to be no reasonable expectation that the singularist's ideal would obtain in real-time terms, he or she contends that one should still hold out the singularist condition as an ideal.

In contrast, the multiplist holds that singularist conditions may obtain in some but not all cases. The multiplist holds that nothing mandates that an interpretation must answer to a singularist ideal. Rather, such ideals are shaped by historically variable circumstances. The multiplist allows that the range of ideally admissible interpretations may be multiple, that the range of competing interpretations need not be conclusively narrowed to a limit of one. The multiplist does not construe rightness in an exclusivist way. On the other hand, while he or she allows that ideally there may be tension between competing interpretations, such tension should be logically weaker than contradiction.[15] The multiplist further allows for nonconclusive grounds for comparing and rationally preferring contending interpretations. The multiplist holds that the standards appropriate for the evaluation of one interpretation might not be fully commensurable with the standards appropriate for the evaluation of another. And importing some overarching standard *in order to* conclusively elim-

---

15. See Göran Hermerén, "The Full Voic'd Quire: Types of Interpretations of Music," in Krausz, *The Interpretation of Music*.

inate all contenders but one might violate the nature of the practice in question. Further, the multiplist holds that this condition reflects no defect. Multiplism is no second-best ideal. Correspondingly, the grounds one might give for preferring one interpretation over another should not be defined so as to beg the question in terms of singularism.

Keeping in mind our discussion of musical interpretation, let us now ramify the multiplist's program. First, as I mentioned, the distinction between admissible and inadmissible interpretations may be sharp or gradual. For example, where one holds that admissible interpretations require strict adherence to all instructions of a score, the distinction between admissible and inadmissible is sharp. But where one holds that the score may arguably be overridden for good reasons, then the distinction between admissible and inadmissible interpretations becomes as gradual as the nature of pertinent reasons will allow. Put otherwise, one could, but need not, take strict adherence to the score as a criterion for separating admissible from inadmissible interpretations. If one does so, though, one should not take such adherence as the grounds for rationally preferring one admissible interpretation over another admissible interpretation. Such judgments would need to be grounded in other sorts of considerations, such as musicianship, expressiveness, or the like. In any event, we should not commit the multiplist to the view that, specifically, strict adherence to the score should separate admissible from inadmissible interpretations. The particular grounds for doing so remain open and contestable. Correspondingly, Muti's remark that sometimes it is a *mistake* to interpret a work of music as strictly notated could mean either that an interpretation which strictly adheres to the score is inadmissible, or that it might be admissible but is not rationally preferred. I take Muti to be affirming the latter view. For the singularist, grounds for rational preference are just the grounds that separate admissible from inadmissible interpretations. Accordingly, he or she would understand Muti's remark to be suggesting that whatever the grounds separating admissible from inadmissible interpretations, they do not include strict adherence to the score. *Yet there are other grounds that do.* Here the putative "mistake" would be admitting as admissible an interpretation which strictly adheres to the score.

Again, the multiplist would hold that the grounds for separating admissible from inadmissible interpretations cannot be the same as the grounds for preferability among admissible interpretations. He or she would understand Muti's remark as suggesting that, *either,* strict nonadherence to the score is necessary for the interpretation to be admissible, and the preferability of remaining admissible interpretations would have to be assessed along other lines; *or,* that Muti is not addressing himself to the criterion for separating admissible from inadmissible interpretations at all; he is not laying down that either strict adherence or nonadherence to the score is a necessary condition for admissibility. Rather, *as a ground for rational preferability,* Muti would be disvaluing strict adherence to the score. Either way, it would be most implausible to suppose that Muti would hold that those interpretations which strictly adhere to the score are, on that account, inadmissible. The general point is that for the multiplist the grounds that separate admissibility from inadmissibility should not be the same as those that distinguish among admissible interpretations.

Second, in the case considered I have addressed whether one should override features of the score that it commands or recommends. Of course, the conditions necessary to override recommendations are correspondingly weaker than those that override commands. In any case, the point that there are nonconverging practices for commands applies as well for recommendations, and such nonconvergence is central to the multiplist's claim.

Third, I have suggested that, although what is specified in a score may be sufficient but perhaps not fully necessary for the identification of a work, it is not sufficient for an interpretation of it. Extra-score practices are required for completing the interpretation. Since these practices may vary, and no one of them can be established as the single right one, the view that there is a single right interpretation must yield to the view that there may be a multiplicity of ideally admissible interpretations of a given work.

Now, along multiplist lines, an interpreter might allow more than one ideally admissible interpretation and still, for good reasons, prefer one interpretation. At the same time, the multiplist could allow that the alternative interpreter might embrace standards independent of his or her own that would license an alternative judgment. And there might be available no further overarching metastandard in virtue of which these substandards could be conclusively ranked.

Yet a singularist might urge further that without some account of works of music which is fully independent of interpretations, one could not hold that an interpretation was or was not "faithful" to the work. The work, according to this argument, should be the touchstone for admissibility. But the admissibility of interpretations *is* constrained by such sufficiently determinate limits as the score in the context of interpretation practices, and no more is required. It is not required that there be a fully autonomous work that is independent of interpretation, if that is a coherent thought at all. (See Part II.)

Fourth, multiplism holds that competing interpretations may be simultaneously admissible and that the standards pertinent to each may be incommensurable. Conceding that competing interpretations may be multiply admissible does not rule out that there may be good reasons for preferring any one of the interpretations in question. Without a commensurating standard between competing interpretations it does not follow that there is no room for critical comparison. *Incommensurability does not entail arbitrariness.*

That competing interpretations may incongruously coexist in the absence of commensurating standards should not be taken as an imperfection, or the result of critical consideration cut short, or anything of the sort. In pertinent cases this coexistence should be taken as fulfilling an ideal condition. Such incommensurability, resulting in *inconclusivity,* arises from no epistemic lack. It is not the case that in the long run, with more information, a singularist condition must obtain. We saw this in the example of the interpretations of Beethoven's First Symphony. There the standards of "faithfulness to the score" and "aesthetic consistency" are incongruent, and there is no available overarching standard which could conclusively rank those standards in turn. Yet, proponents of each interpretation may urge the appropriateness of their interpretation. They may provide good, though inconclusive, reasons for their interpretation. With respect to each standard, in turn, one interpretation may be thought to be preferable over the other.

Fifth, highly personalized interpretations, such as those of conductors Willem Mengelberg or Leopold Stokowski, might prompt the singularist to pursue a "pluralizing" strategy in order to install a singularist condition. The singularist might argue along the following lines: concede the multiplicity of interpretive practices, but bifurcate the object-of-interpretation. That is, construe each admissible interpretation as ideal *for a given occasion*. The interpretive practices then in place would mandate one and only one ideally admissible interpretation. That other practices on other occasions lead to other singular ideal interpretations would be allowable too. Put otherwise, a full description of interpretive practices on a given occasion would mandate the single right interpretation for that occasion. On another occasion another full description of interpretive practices would mandate another single right interpretation. But one result of such a strategy would be that these interpretations on different occasions could not be interpretations of the same work of music.

As a general strategy this extreme pluralizing maneuver will not go through, since, as I shall argue in Chapter 2, the very idea of a range of ideally admissible interpretations—whether singularist or multiplist—is predicated on the idea of a practice construed as a social rather than an individual phenomenon. As a function of practices, the range of ideally admissible interpretations is socially constituted over historical time. A practice is consensually sanctioned by appropriate practitioners. A practice is not comprised by a particular person at an instant. And while there must always be a collection of persons in a social group, the rules, guidelines and values of a practice are not embodied in any one or specific number of particular individuals in the group. So, there can be no such thing as a single-person, single-occasion practice. This is an important constraint on singularists who seek to dismantle putatively multiplist cases by distributing admissible interpretations over works of music pluralized to individual persons or occasions. So seen, the idea of a single-person, single-occasion practice would be an oxymoron; it undercuts the essentially social character of practices as such.

To reiterate, an ideally admissible interpretation is not fully notated in a characteristically incomplete score. Extra-score considerations are required for completing interpretations. Although what is specified in a score is not sufficient for an interpretation of it, what is specified in a score may be sufficient—but perhaps not fully necessary—for the identification of the work of music. So, if there is a multiplicity of ideally admissible interpretive practices, it is a mistake to assume that there must be a single ideally admissible interpretation. There is a certain latitude between what is interpreted and what is notated as instruction in a score. The difference between what is interpreted and what is notated is "the score-in-the-context-of-its-interpretation-practices." Within this latitude is the room for interpretation. Here extra-score considerations enter which are required for an admissible interpretation of the work. In this way, as an entrenched classical genre, scores as such are in the relevant sense incomplete. Where extra-score interpretive practices vary, and where there are no univocal and overarching standards in virtue of which a number of competing interpretation practices may be conclusively ranked, there can be no single ideal interpretation. To insist that the range of ideally admissible interpretations must always be singular is to violate an entrenched feature of classical interpretations, namely the incompleteness of scores in relation to the multiplicity of interpretation practices.

The Singularist's Appeal to an Ontology of Real Works of Music

I have tried to avoid speaking about the multiplicity of interpretations in relation to works of music as opposed to scores, leaving open the question of the relation between works of music and scores. Indeed, throughout this study I shall remain agnostic about the ontology of cultural entities generally. But there is a strategy that the singularist might deploy which implicates such a connection between works of music and interpretations.

The singularist might appeal directly to a putatively determinate work of music, one *independent* of interpretation practices as such, which mandates a single right interpretation of it. Now, I shall resist appeals to an ontological realist entity which is thought to reside independent of interpretation practices as such. As I shall argue in Part II, there is no reason to believe that one could have access to such entities. Further, there is no reason to assume that such entities need present themselves with sufficient determinacy to perform the task of constraining admissible interpretations to a limit of one.

The kind of ontological realism such singularists would embrace is insufficient to insure their singularist condition. Indeed, such a realism would be compatible with either singularism or multiplism, and so it would be neutral with respect to singularism or multiplism. As well, ontological constructionism will also be found to be compatible with either singularism or multiplism. Consequently, the question of ideality and the question of ontology will be found to be logically detachable.

The ontological realist view in music is by no means unrepresented. Consider, for example, the suggestions of Morris Grossman, Nicholas Wolterstorff, and Karl Popper. Grossman speaks of the need for something transcendent in relation to which musical fidelity can be made intelligible. "A Beethoven sonata exists as a physical score and as a series of performances. But it also exists as an abstract or ideal notion of its correct rendition. We cannot talk about an obligation to accuracy without generating the idea of prior existence and correctness." Grossman goes on to say: "The true Sonata, the Platonic form, prior and subsequent to his efforts, was likely something poor, deaf Beethoven was loath to think he could approach. Seen this way, performance is a continuation of a search, not the presentation of a settled discovery. A performance is not so much a member of a class as a longing for an impossible way of being."[16]

It is interesting to note that while Grossman holds that the true sonata, the Platonic form, exists prior to and subsequent to Beethoven's efforts, Beethoven himself could not approach it. But there is no reason to assume that the continuation of the search would issue in any settled work in relation to which a single right interpretation of it would be made out. On Grossman's own account, we have no

---

16. Maurice Grossman, "Performance and Obligation," in Alperson, *What Is Music?*, pp. 279–80.

access to the work in relation to which admissible interpretions could be adjudicated. Rather, Grossman's ontological realism derives from the motivational point that without some posited though inaccessible entity, the very idea of interpretive admissibility cannot be made out. But such admissibility can be sufficiently constrained by historically conditioned interpretation practices.

In turn, Nicholas Wolterstorff is motivated by a distinct view of freedom when he posits musical works as transcendental objects. He says:

> In short, around autonomous art we have constructed an ideology in which such art is seen as transcending the alienation of everyday society. To immerse oneself in a work of art is to enter a higher realm—a realm of freedom and transcendent universality: freedom from social demands alien to the artist, transcending the particularity of the artist's society so as to put us in touch with universal humanity. Our picturing of the artist as socially oblivious is an unavoidable corollary of his ideology. If freedom and universality are principally what one looks for in art, then the embodiment in art of social reality will never catch one's eye.... And if, finally, we ask why we in the modern West have felt impelled to see in art something transcending the bondage and particularity of society, imparting to us a glimpse of nonalienated existence, of humanity at home on earth and in society, then no doubt part of the answer will have to consist of taking note of the fact that as the Christian religion lost its grip on the minds and hearts of Western humanity, some filled the gap with faith in the present and future wonders of science and technology, while others filled it with Art—art understood now as *opera perfecta et absoluta*.[17]

Wolterstorff's remarks are directed to art works in general and to musical works in particular. While Grossman concedes that we may not have access to his posited transcendental entities, Wolterstorff suggests that we may indeed be "in touch with" his posited transcendental entities and thereby with "universal humanity." And such access is to be understood in the terms of Christian faith.

---

17. Nicholas Wolterstorff, "The Work of Making a Work of Music," in Alperson, *What Is Music?*, p. 128.

Now, even if one were to concede that the idea of such transcendental entities is intelligible, and even if one were to concede that one could have access to them, there is no reason to believe that they would be sufficiently determinate so as to constrain the range of ideally admissible interpretations of them to a limit of one.

Consider yet another ontological realist's view of works of music. Karl Popper distinguishes objective music from subjective music.[18] Objective music is exemplified in the works of J. S. Bach, where the musician is seen as "struggling to solve musical problems." Subjective music is exemplified in the works of Beethoven and more extremely in the works of Wagner, where the musician is seen as "engaged in expressing emotions." The task of writing a minuet or trio, especially when its problem-situation is presented by a half-completed suite carrying its own structural requirements, is very different in kind from that of expressing one's emotions. Popper opts for objective music as fully bona fide, for the satisfactoriness of a work is, on his view, a function of its ability to resolve its problem-situation. In subjective music, where problem-situations are less definable if at all, resolutions are less definable, and so grounds for evaluation are correspondingly illusive. Without a clearly defined problem-situation, there can be no standards in terms of which the quality of work could be judged. In short, for Popper, the more subjective, the less criticizable. If subjective music is music it is of a degenerate kind.

Popper's concern with the critical function leads him more generally to criticize expressionist theories of art, which he thinks are unconcerned with objective problem-situations above and beyond the discharge of unbridled emotions. He argues that such theories are empty of content, since they tell us nothing distinctive of art. After all, all forms of sentient activity are expressive. Popper says:

> For everything a man or an animal can do is... an expression of internal states of emotion and of a personality. This is trivially true for all kinds of humans and animal languages. It holds for the way a man or a lion walks, the way a man coughs or blows his nose, the way a man or a lion may look at you or ignore you. It holds

---

18. Karl Popper, *Unended Quest: An Intellectual Autobiography* (LaSalle, Ill.: Open Court, 1976), pp. 60–68.

for the way a bird builds its nest, a spider constructs its web, and a man builds his house. In other words, it is not a characteristic of art.[19]

Popper locates works of music in his so-called World 3, as entities with objective contents. Popper distinguishes between three types of entities: physical states, which occupy World 1, subjective or mental or belief states, which occupy World 2, and objective contents of thoughts or intelligibles, which occupy World 3. World 3 entities include, among other things, true and false scientific theories, mathematical or logical postulates and theorems, and the objective contents of artworks including works of music. While World 3 entities arise from conditions of Worlds 1 and 2, they transcend such conditions. Popper is explicit about his Platonic characterization of World 3 entities as regards their autonomous nature. What distinguishes Popper from Plato, according to his own account, is that while Plato held that "intelligibles" exist timelessly in both the directions of past and future, Popper holds that the "intelligibles" may be genuinely created at a particular time, before which they did not exist. Problem-situations and their resolutions in music, as in science, are brought into existence at a particular time, but then they continue to exist timelessly. And, once they are brought into existence, they are in principle reconstructable, should their World 1 or World 2 embodiments cease to exist. Popper allows that a work of music is brought into existence under certain historical conditions within the context of definable interpretive practices. Yet it transcends such conditions. Again, as in the arguments made by Grossman and Wolterstorff, whether or not we may have access to such third worldly entities independently of the context of interpretive practices in particular historically defined circumstances, there is no reason to believe that such entities would be sufficiently determinate so as to be able to adjudicate between contending musical interpretations. The existence of such posited entities seem incapable of narrowing the range of ideally admissible interpretations to a limit of one.

19. Ibid., p. 62.

Musical Practice instead of Ontology

The view here favored is not concerned to offer a particular theory of the ontology of works of music, nor, as I shall argue, will we need one. For present purposes the understanding of musical interpretation should begin not with a realist view of works of music, but rather with an understanding of musical practice. Whichever posture one favors regarding the ontology of works of music, one cannot make musical phenomena intelligible independently of the historically constituted practices in which they are found and fostered. In a similar vein Roger Scruton assigns priority to musical practice:

> The rules of music are summaries of musical practice. To make them prescriptive is to kill the process whereby they themselves are made. On the other hand, to abolish them at a sweep, is to abolish the musical culture, and therefore the musical understanding, which would make their abolition intelligible... a musical culture does not exist *in addition* to the music which compels it. The culture creates the music which creates it, by providing the only conditions under which composition is possible, or under which the work of music can be heard.[20]

Let us now more fully consider the very idea of a practice that functions as the matrix in terms of which we should understand the singularist and multiplist ideals.

---

20. Roger Scruton, "Musical Understanding and Musical Culture," in Alperson, *What Is Music?*, p. 358.

2

Cultural Practices and the Ideals of Interpretation: Singularism and Multiplism

The very ideas of singularism and multiplism rest upon the idea of a practice. Before turning to a more systematic characterization of singularism and multiplism, let us consider the idea of a practice.

Practices

Keeping practices of musical interpretations in mind, we may say generally that a practice provides the aims and orientations of its programs, and these enter into the evaluation of appropriate products.[1] A practice thereby provides the terms in which the range of ideally admissible solutions to its problem-situations is coherently adoptable. Practices orient practitioners as to what features of their domain of inquiry are significant or salient. They provide values in virtue of which certain sorts of problem-situations and solutions are countenanced as legitimate and fruitful. Their rules, guidelines, values, or procedures indicate appropriate methods, maneuvers, and scope

---

1. We should distinguish the present sense of practice from another very general sense of practice which is sometimes associated with Wittgenstein's idea of a form of life. The latter does not function criterially in that it does not determine which specific interpretations are appropriate for a given domain.

of works to be pursued within them. Further, the character of a practice is set within the context of its pursuit, which involves the realization of its aims as well as its continual reformulation in light of its achievements.

The range of ideally admissible interpretations is that range of interpretations of a given object-of-interpretation that is deemed ideally admissible by informed practitioners in the pertinent sense.[2] Because it is a function of a practice, the range of ideally admissible interpretations is socially constituted. It is not important which particular individuals enter into such relations, but rather *that* such relations obtain. While there must always be a collection of individual persons in a social group, the rules, guidelines, values, or procedures of a practice are not embodied in any one or number of particular individuals in the group. This does not mean, as José Ferrater-Mora says:

> a consensus is reached by vote counting, or by tyrannical rule, or by more or less "authoritarian" and "authoritative" influences—even if this is just what sometimes happens. No matter how much one argues, reasons, computes, or appeals to empirical data formulated in an observational language—which, by the way, may itself be the subject of some "consensus"—what in the last resort makes a proposition acceptable or not is the consensus, or agreement, that it is, indeed, acceptable or not. This consensus functions within the rules laid down, implicitly or explicitly, by the community of researchers by virtue of habits engendered by a multitude of common experiences.[3]

Since the range of ideally admissible interpretations is a function of its place in a given practice, and since a practice is consensually defined, so the range of ideally admissible interpretations is consensually defined. (This point will be further refined later in Part I.) Singularism and multiplism are intelligible as *praxial* ideals—that is,

---

2. I coin the phrase "object-of-interpretation" as a term of art to signal that no particular ontological construal of that which is interpreted is thereby implied. It remains ontologically neutral. I shall discuss this issue more fully in Part II.

3. José Ferrater-Mora, "On Practice," *American Philosophical Quarterly* 13 (January 1976), 51–52.

as ideals within certain practices—and the adoptability of either is a function of the particular practices in which they appear.

Correspondingly, disallowing "individual" single-person or single-occasion "practices" is an important constraint on those who would seek to dismantle a putatively multiplist case by pluralizing (as I shall say) an object-of-interpretation to range over would-be individual practices. Such pluralizing to "individual practices" is an oxymoron; it undercuts the social character of practice as such. (We encountered this possibility in Chapter 1 when considering musical interpreters Willem Mengelberg and Leopold Stokowski.) In sum, the very idea of a range of ideally admissible interpretation is predicated on a practice as a social rather than a person-specific or occasion-specific condition of ideality.

The judgment whether singularism or multiplism is an appropriate ideal for a given practice requires that one has sufficient information about the pertinent practice. At the same time, there is no algorithmic or formal set of procedures to determine whether a practice's rules, guidelines, values, or procedures are being satisfied, since these operate in rather loose ways. They function as varying clusters of informal and nonfixed constraints. Thus, there are no mechanical procedures to test whether complete knowledge about the practice has been obtained, since the limits of practices are not determinate. Yet judgments about sufficiency of knowledge are made informally, largely along the lines of those provided by informed practitioners, based, as Ferrater-Mora says, upon "a multitude of common experiences." An informed practitioner can judge whether information is sufficient to say whether one or another praxial ideal is appropriate. In this way, the notion of sufficiency of information falls back upon the notion of consensus by informed practitioners.

One can violate a practice by imposing a praxial ideal that the nature of the study at hand does not admit. Of course, there is no a priori reason why a given practice ought not be violated. One can imagine that, on specific occasions, good reasons for doing so might be provided. Put otherwise, there is nothing sacrosanct about practices as received, but special reasons above and beyond one's prior commitment to a particular praxial ideal should be offered on a piecemeal basis. In any case, the onus of the argument is on the one who proposes to change the character of a received practice.

Singularism and Multiplism: A Note on Terms

Now let us consider a more formal characterization of singularism, multiplism, and their respective strategies. A word about terminology is in order. The issues that I have raised regarding praxial ideality have been raised before by authors who have used different terms. For example, Wayne Booth, David Hoy, and Alexander Nehamas are among those who use "critical monism" roughly for my singularism, and "critical pluralism" roughly for my multiplism.[4] David Hoy, for example, in characterizing his distinction between critical monist and critical pluralist, says, "Critical monism is the view that all the questions about all the features of a text must be postulated as being resolvable, at least at the ideal limit. Critical pluralism is a response to this view, and maintains that monism represents philosophical overkill. For pluralists, disagreements can be reasonable without necessarily being resolvable. Dissent can be rational without presupposing ideal convergence or consensus."[5]

I adopt the distinction between singularist and multiplist instead of the one between critical monist and critical pluralist because my distinction will help to bring into relief the question of the identity of objects-of-interpretation. Specifically, while the distinction between the critical monist and the critical pluralist concerns whether there should be one or more ideally admissible interpretations, assuming the commonality or "unicity" of an object-of-interpretation among contending interpretations, I wish to thematize questions concerning just such commonality. Therefore I reserve "pluralist" to designate a specific maneuver that transforms otherwise multiplist conditions into singularist ones. I shall more fully address this pluralizing maneuver after considering a more formal characterization of singularism and multiplism.

---

4. Wayne Booth, *Critical Understanding: The Powers and Limits of Pluralism* (Chicago: University of Chicago Press, 1979); David Couzens Hoy, "Dworkin's Constructive Optimism v. Deconstructive Legal Nihilism," *Law and Philosophy* 6 (1987), 321–56. Alexander Nehamas, "The Postulated Author: Critical Monism as a Regulative Ideal," *Critical Inquiry* 8 (Autumn 1981), 133–49.

5. Hoy, "Dworkin's Constructive Optimism," 351.

Singularism   Multiplism

I - 1   I - 1   I - 2

O - 1   O - 1

Singularist Condition: For any object-of-interpretation, there is one and only one ideally admissible interpretation of it.

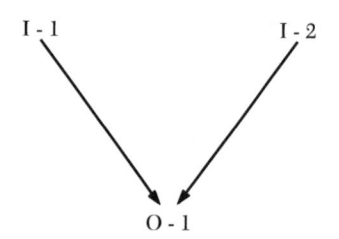

Multiplist Condition: For some object-of-interpretation, there is more than one ideally admissible interpretation of it.

Illustration 3. Singularism and multiplism

Singularism

Singularists hold that, for a given object-of-interpretation, the range of ideally competing interpretations should be conclusively narrowed to a limit of one; and that the range of ideally admissible interpretations in all practices should be singular. They construe rightness in an exclusivist way, and take the rightness of a given interpretation to be logically incompatible with the rightness of alternative interpretations. The singularist holds that the singularist condition is inherently more rational than the multiplist condition. Being universal, the singularist's claim is refutable by the instantiation of practices in which the singularist's ideal is misplaced.

Singularists are motivated by the assumption that the most satisfactory end of an informed discussion of competing interpretations is one in which there is full convergence or consensus according to a single agreed upon standard. Thus they require that the single right interpretation should conclusively unseat alternative interpretations. (There will be more about conclusivity later in this chapter.) Even if, for a particular practice, there seems to be no reasonable expectation that the singularist's ideal would obtain in real-time terms, the singularist contends that one should still hold out singularism as an ideal.

The singularist's ideal is characteristically embraced in a certain tradition in the philosophy of science. There, it is urged, one's inability to capture the single right interpretation on a given occasion should not deter one from holding out a singularist aim. For example, following a broadly Popperian approach, Ian Jarvie puts the point succinctly:

> We must assume that there is such a thing as truth and aim at it if we are to have a progressive science. We should not worry that we can never know for certain when we have truth. Worry is unnecessary because there is something like a criterion which tells us that we are approaching it. This criterion is the discovery, and thereby the elimination, of some of our past errors. Although our ignorance is infinite, it is some achievement that we have detected and eliminated such qualities of errors in our theories.[6]

Put otherwise, state Q is progressive over state P if it more nearly approximates an ideally projected state Z. On this view, science should aim for the unfulfillable ideal of singular truth, which explains progress in the history of science and motivates the practice of science as it unfolds.

The multiplist may or may not embrace the singularist's aim in natural science. But even there the multiplist may observe that singularism is not necessary in order to account for a minimal notion of progress. Indeed, singularism is not mandated by a method of error elimination for which Karl Popper is justly famous. In the above quotation, for example, Jarvie says that one can never know for certain that one has discovered the truth, but it remains unclear whether the ideal condition of the inquiry must be singular. The method of error elimination still applies if one allows that the range of ideally admissible interpretations is not singular. Singularism is no requirement for the idea of growth. The ideal results of error elimination need not be the conclusive overthrow of all but one competing interpretation. Put otherwise, the multiplist allows that state Q would be progressive over state P if Q more nearly approximates *either* X, Y, or Z—these latter states in turn not being conclusively rankable.

---

6. Ian Jarvie, *The Revolution in Anthropology* (London: Routledge and Kegan Paul, 1964), pp. 16–17.

Multiplism

In contrast, leaving aside the question whether natural science is a cultural practice, the multiplist allows that the range of ideally admissible interpretations in some practices should be multiple; that the range of competing interpretations for a given object-of-interpretation should not be conclusively narrowed to a limit of one. As I have anticipated in Chapter 1, multiplism is compatible with singularist conditions in some practices, but singularism is incompatible with multiplist conditions in any practice. The multiplist does not construe rightness in an exclusivist way. He or she allows that the tension between two competing interpretations may be logically weaker than contradiction or exclusivity. The multiplist allows for nonconclusive grounds for comparing and rationally preferring contending interpretations.

Indeed, the standards appropriate for the evaluation of one interpretation might not be fully commensurable with the standards appropriate for the evaluation of the other. And importing some overarching standard *in order to* conclusively eliminate all contenders but one might violate the nature of the practice in question. Multiplism is motivated by a skepticism about the singularist's claim that in principle there are always metastandards in virtue of which one can conclusively adjudicate between competing interpretations. The multiplist is motivated by the conviction that there are cases of competing interpretations that are not fully commensurable.

While rightness and wrongness (or admissibility and inadmissibility) exclude each other, it does not follow that what is not wrong (or not inadmissible) is singularly right (or admissible). One might suggest that the thought that there could be a multiplicity of right interpretations of a given object-of-interpretation grates against ordinary language usage. But there seems nothing strained about saying that there is no *one* right way. If one were to route a trip from New York City to Los Angeles, for example, one might recommend going via Chicago or Denver. Both would be right or admissible. Surely it would be wrong or inadmissible to go eastward to London. Of course, one might "strengthen the demands" by introducing further conditions of speed, convenience, interestingness, scenery, comfort of ride, and so on. But these additions would change the aim. The aim would no longer be just to get to Los Angeles, but to do so under certain revised conditions. In any case, in the absence of the strengthened demands, there seems no violation to ordinary language to say that there may be several right or admissible ways.

The multiplist holds that there is no reason to hold out a singularist ideal where the analysis of a particular practice is such that it resists such an ideal. Multiplism is no second best ideal. Rather than think of multiplist conditions as being always en route to an ideal singularist condition (which they may sometimes be), the multiplist allows that a singularist condition may itself be interim or en route to a yet deeper understanding of the complexities of pertinent practices. Indeed, on this view, the fact that the singularist condition might have been achieved is no guarantee that all pertinent considerations would have been taken into account, nor that, under ideal conditions, the discussion is over. Full convergence toward a single interpretation is no mark that an ideal condition has been attained.

What divides the singularist from the multiplist is not just an epistemic difference. It is not that—on the assumption that in principle there always is a single right interpretation—one holds that such an interpretation is always accessible and the other holds that sometimes it is not. Rather the difference is deeper. While the singularist holds that there is always a single right interpretation (which is sometimes accessible and sometimes not), the multiplist holds that sometimes there just is no single right interpretation.

A Singularist Reply: Strengthen Demands

The singularist might reply to the multiplist: make singular the multiple; make conclusive the inconclusive. If two interpretations appear to be admissible according to different standards, the singularist could urge that one should strengthen demands by introducing further scale-tipping standards.[7] This scale-tipping strategy is meant to disqualify conclusively all but one overriding standard, and thereby all

---

7. See Larry Briskman, *Problems and Their Progress: Toward a Sceptical Theory of Scientific Inquiry*, Ph.D. dissertation, University of Edinburgh, 1983; see also Ronald Dworkin, *A Matter of Principle* (Oxford: Clarendon Press, 1986).

but one interpretation. The added standard is supposed to guarantee conclusiveness. Scale-tipping added standards should emerge, it might be suggested, by attending more closely to the details of the case, by filling in a fuller description of it, by situating it within a larger context, or the like.[8] This, the singularist holds, is always an open option. In response to the multiplist's claim that in certain cases no more standards should be expected, the singularist asks us to keep looking.

Put otherwise, where interpretation A may be better than interpretation B with respect to standard S_1, and where interpretation B may be better than interpretation A with respect to S_2, one may hold that one should strengthen demands by assigning greater weight to S_1, say, over S_2 (or vice versa) by importing a scale-tipping overarching standard which values interpretation A over B (or vice versa). According to this strategy, it is always the case that S_1 and S_2 can be ranked by some overarching standard. So, there can be no genuine cases of incommensurability.

The singularist, then, holds that such a method of strengthening demands is an option that is always formally available. One can always conclusively rank lower-level standards by invoking some such overarching standard as general as, for example: the most coherent, unified, perspicuous, illuminating, or something of the sort. Such very general sorts of standards are supposed to "resolve" apparent multiplisms.

But if we keep in mind such cases as the competing interpretations of Beethoven's First Symphony, such supposed overarching standards are characteristically too general or vague or equivocal to function in the criterialogical way required. For example, one might plausibly hold that either Muti's or Comissiona's interpretation was more coherent, unified, perspicuous, illuminating, and so forth. But attempts to sharpen these standards to make them function critically runs the risk of begging the question. The deployment of such very general overarching standards—if they can still be called standards—for the conclusive ranking of interpretations is problematic.

8. Dworkin, *A Matter of Principle*. In legal interpretation, for example, Dworkin holds that one may strengthen demands by introducing added standards from neighboring subfields in the law. One might generalize this strategy (as Dworkin does not) by suggesting that standards may be strengthened by appealing to neighboring disciplines such as history or political philosophy.

The method of strengthening demands is not *always* an open option. Sometimes it is unreasonable to "keep looking" or to "extend the discussion" by turning to neighboring fields, since, if after the method of strengthening demands were initially applied and yet further multiplisms obtained, the method would need to be applied again and again. If, for example, a multiplism in legal interpretation were sought to be "resolved" by strengthening demands from political theory, and then there were to arise other multiplisms within this expanded complex, presumably the method would need to be reapplied to strengthen demands from, say, economics, and so on. But there would seem to be no terminus to such a maneuver. Correspondingly, if a multiplism in musical interpretation, for example, were "resolved" by strengthening demands borrowed from folklore, and then there arose other multiplisms within this expanded complex, the method would need to be reapplied, borrowing from, say, the history of dance, and so on. Again, there would seem to be no terminus to such a maneuver. One could not be reasonably assured that appropriate limits of the inquiry had been sufficiently inventoried. The end of inquiry may be perpetually deferred. To be sure, the method of strengthening demands by expanding a problematic horizon may well go far toward disqualifying some interpretations. But the singularist requires that some such method be always formally available. Yet, no matter how widely one might cast the evidential net—no matter how richly the evidence may be described—it may still underdetermine any one single interpretation.

The Appeal to Intentions

As a strategy for identifying a pertinent overarching standard, the singularist might be tempted to appeal to the original intention of the creator of an object-of-interpretation. Yet this suggestion runs into several problems. First, there are epistemological difficulties in recovering the original intentions of creators. Second, the individual creator might well have had essentially ambiguous or incongruous intentions. Third, for those products which were collectively rather than individually created, it is unclear where one should look for intentions. And fourth, a work may embody features that the creator—whether individual or collective—never intended. Indeed, cultural objects are characteristically emergent in the sense that their finished character often embodies properties that are unintended by their creator. This means that, at least with respect to those emergent properties, the creator carries no special status as one to assign salience or significance or meaning. So, the intentions of a creator need not locate or exhaust ideally admissible interpretations of a work. For these sorts of reasons, the original intentions of a creator do not guarantee the singularist's requirement.

We should note that the distinction between singularist and multiplist is not coextensive with the distinction between intentionalist and anti-intentionalist. The disagreement between intentionalists such as E. D. Hirsch and anti-intentionalists such as Monroe Beardsley is not a disagreement over singularism and multiplism.[9] They both embrace singularism. They disagree, however, about the sorts of constraints appropriate for eliminating all but one ideally admissible interpretation. In turn, multiplist counterarguments may well be turned against either intentionalists or anti-intentionalists. However interesting and important the differences between them, Beardsley and Hirsch agree that, with respect to a given object-of-interpretation, ideally there should be full convergence toward a single interpretation with no logical tension. Of them Joseph Margolis says that they favor "exclusively correct and comprehensive interpretations; but none has shown why non-converging interpretations cannot be legitimately defended."[10]

Now, in light of these considerations, as I anticipated in Chapter 1, a singularist might propose that one should *postulate* a creator—perhaps not to coincide with the historical creator—in relation to which ideally admissible interpretations should be determined.[11] The postulated creator would be an idealized creator whose gaze would be constructed based upon the created work as received within the context of appropriate interpretive practices. He or she would be a rational reconstruction

---

9. E. D. Hirsch, *Validity in Interpretation* (New Haven: Yale University Press, 1976). See, for example, W. K. Wimsatt, Jr., and Monroe Beardsley, "The Intentional Fallacy," in Wimsatt, *The Verbal Icon: Studies in the Meaning of Poetry* (Lexington: University of Kentucky Press, 1954). See also Monroe Beardsley, *The Possibility of Criticism* (Detroit: Wayne State University Press, 1970).
10. Joseph Margolis, *Art and Philosophy* (Atlantic Highlands, N.J.: Humanities Press, 1980), p. 157.
11. See, for example, Nehamas, "The Postulated Author."

of a creator whose intentions—were he or she to have actually created the work—could best make sense of the work as received. And he or she would be a creator in relation to whose postulated intentions competing interpretations could be adjudicated in a conclusive way.

Difficulty with this suggestion arises when considering what is involved in postulating a creator. To start with, what an interpreter takes as salient or significant in the background information—the work and its surrounding interpretive practices—is already multiply interpretable. As I have said, the background information is characteristically such that no one creator is mandated, and more than one may be plausibly postulated. Further, in the rational construction of a postulated creator, what interpreters take as rational may vary. It follows, therefore, that, consistent with the same background information, more than one creator may be postulated.

The singularist's temptation to appeal to the intentions of a postulated creator parallels his or her temptation to appeal to ontologically real entities. But, as I shall argue more fully in Part II, ontological questions are logically detachable from the question of praxial ideality. Specifically, whether one embraces an ontological realism or an ontological constructionism with respect to pertinent objects-of-interpretation is logically independent of the question of singularism versus multiplism. Since neither singularism nor multiplism entails either ontological realism or ontological constructionism, and since neither ontological realism nor ontological constructionism entails either singularism or multiplism, neither ontological realism nor ontological constructionism explains why we should embrace either singularism or multiplism. Correspondingly, there is no reason to believe that the intentions of a postulated creator (in this context, the analogue of ontologically real entities) must be such as to constrain the range of ideally admissible interpretations to a limit of one.

Multiplism and Interpretive Anarchy

If singularism is sometimes too strong, is multiplism then too weak? In other words, what prevents the multiplist's position from lapsing into a kind of interpretive anarchy? What constraints are there on the multiplist's range of ideally admissible interpretations? Particular constraints are specific to the practices in question. They depend upon what the practice and its informed practitioners lay down as pertinent rules, guidelines, values, procedures, or the like. There is no general answer to the question of what constraints resist an "anything goes" anarchism. Yet we may say more than this.

Conceding that competing interpretations may be multiply admissible does not rule out that there may be good reasons for preferring any one of the interpretations in question. The absence of a commensurating standard between competing interpretations does not entail that there is no room for critical comparison. *Incommensurability does not entail irrationality or abitrariness.* Incommensurability allows for comparability and rational preferability.

At this juncture we may observe that the logical condition of inconclusiveness should not be confused with the psychological condition of indecisiveness—an attitude with which one might actually embrace a certain interpretation. Conclusiveness is a logical notion, and decisiveness is a psychological notion. That is, grounds for rationally preferring one interpretation over its other admissible competitors may be inconclusive (because it might be incommensurable with its competitors), but one may decisively and rationally champion it over its competitors. This distinction is important in the context of the rational preferability of one among a number of admissible interpretations.

In turn, we may ask what, on the multiplist's model, might distinguish multiply admissible interpretations from inadmissible interpretations. Our discussion of the postulated composer in Chapter 1 provides a clue. There I suggested that deviation from the score of Beethoven's First Symphony may be rationally preferred over strict adherence to the score because good reasons could be given for it, and good reasons could make plausible the claim that the resultant interpretation is still an interpretation of Beethoven's First Symphony. Such good reasons would be couched in the rational reconstructability of the overall project in which the question of interpretation arises. To put it otherwise, we may say that an admissible interpretation is constrained by a community of informed practitioners in a position to articulate a reasonable story about the relation of the proposed interpretation to the tradition in which the object-of-interpretation resides. Such articulation is by no means an arbitrary affair. It involves accommodating the salient features of the tradition of the object-of-interpretation, and need not accommodate the specific intentions of the individual historical creator. Rational reconstructability is here understood in social rather than individual terms.

Conductor Roger Norrington, for example, interprets the nine symphonies of Beethoven with period instruments to recapture the style of the orchestra that Beethoven had available to him. This effort is meant to accommodate, if not Beethoven's intentions, then at least the musical culture of Beethoven's time. Yet Riccardo Muti justifies interpreting the Beethoven symphonies with a contemporary orchestra with the suggestion that Beethoven would have been most pleased to incorporate intervening instrumental and ensemble innovations. For example, Muti says,

> personally I prefer the use of modern instruments for these composers, because the modern instruments, generally speaking—with exceptions of course—represent an improvement in the quality of the sound. The contrabassi today make a better and bigger sound that is certainly much more helpful for certain composers. And today we are used to hearing, for example, Beethoven's Ninth Symphony with a huge chorus, a large orchestra, double woodwinds, and so on. Certainly, we create a sound Beethoven didn't have in mind. But if you see the autographed copy of Beethoven's manuscript, and see all the crescendi and fortissimos written by his hand with a red pencil in a very dramatic way, that is, he couldn't imagine the sound that we have today. But the power that he felt and wanted to express is certainly of a normal human being. The fact that these people belonged to a different century doesn't mean that their feelings were different from our feelings today.[12]

To Muti it is evident that Beethoven would have welcomed intervening developments as improvements. But it would be misleading to say (and Muti does not) that the historical Beethoven intended that his work should be interpreted as Muti and other conductors of modern orchestras do.

At the same time, Norrington's interpretations of the Beethoven symphonies are interesting, not so much because they can claim to

---

12. Riccardo Muti, in an interview conducted by the author at the American Society for Aesthetics–Eastern Division, Philadelphia, April 21, 1989.

have recaptured the way Beethoven actually intended his music (which Norrington does not say), but because they capture the orchestra of Beethoven's time. Further, they are interesting in light of the intervening development of the modern orchestra. Contemporary audiences have largely come to know Beethoven's symphonies with the modern orchestra in their mind's ear. And it is in relation to that history that the Norrington symphonies are interesting. Further, Norrington's interpretations provide musical clues for appreciating musical elements that the concert listener might not otherwise appreciate. Yet we cannot claim to retrieve the musical historical past, for given intervening developments, we cannot regain the lost innocence of our mind's ear. Accordingly, Muti undercuts the idea of recreating the musical experience of audiences of Beethoven's time.

Muti acknowledges as much:

> using the original instruments you cannot say you are capturing the original intentions of the composer. The entire life has changed. ... The musicians arrive in the city by plane. They go to the hall by car. They eat and drink in a different way, and they dress in a different way. They have halls that are bigger with chairs covered with velvet and are very comfortable. At the time of Mozart it was only wood. The chairs and theatres were much more simple. They didn't have all the plush that we have today for the comfort and pleasure of today's public. And the sound was different. Even the wigs in the audience of 200 people created an absorption of the sound.... So it's the entire life that is changed. You cannot say, "I will do everything I need to do as a man of today, but I will use old instruments and so I have the right to say that I am recreating the world of Mozart." ... The entire situation is completely different. So I personally thank these colleagues of mine who believe in original instruments. I personally have learned many things from them and they have made an important contribution. But I don't believe that is the only way to make music.[13]

Generally, the admissibility of Muti's and Norrington's interpretations of the Beethoven symphonies is constrained by the reasonableness of the reconstructable accounts of the traditions from which the object-of-interpretation arose. Such a tradition makes the object-of-interpretation intelligible to start with. At the same time, there is

13. Ibid.

no reason to assume that any one rationally reconstructable account is exclusively right. The intentions of any single person—even of the composer—are not conclusive. Rather, such reasonableness depends upon the context of the tradition in which the cultural object arises and is made intelligible. And that context is social. Yet, because such traditions are themselves not foundationally fixed, their accounts must be continually rationally reconstructed. Of course, the terms of such intelligibility may change over time, but not in an arbitrary manner, for they are constrained by the ability of the revised account to make the changes in the pertinent traditions intelligible and reasonable.

The disagreement between Norrington and Muti are about different accommodations of the social context of the object-of-interpretation. This book is not the place to settle their specific dispute. Rather, the example is meant to provide a sense of what such accounts might look like, and to show that they are not arbitrary. There is no conclusive way to settle the dispute, but that does not mean that the preference for one rational reconstruction over another is arbitrary.

We should note that this rational reconstructionist suggestion is neutral with respect to historical conservatism, liberalism, or radicalism, since conservative, liberal, or radical departures from tradition all must make sense of themselves in light of the traditions and histories from which they may depart. In this regard we should be mindful that at a given time a community of "informed" practitioners may not be sufficiently informed to be able to anticipate that at a subsequent time reasonable supporting grounds for an interpretive innovation might be forthcoming. The revised verdict would have to await a yet more informed community of practitioners.

Admissible and Inadmissible Interpretations

Consider further the distinction between admissible and inadmissible interpretations. Logically, one should first separate admissible from inadmissible interpretations, and then proceed to consider the merits of the remaining admissible interpretations. For the multiplist, the grounds for inconclusively comparing admissible interpretations should not be the same as those for separating admissible from inadmissible interpretations. The multiplist should not collapse grounds for rational comparability between admissible interpretations with grounds for separating admissible from inadmissible interpretations. If he or she does, less preferred interpretations would turn out to be inadmissible, and that result would be too strong. For the singularist, on the other hand, the grounds for comparing interpretations just *are* the grounds for separating admissible from inadmissible interpretations.

As I have indicated, the distinction between admissible and inadmissible interpretations may be sharp or gradual. For example, where one holds that admissible musical interpretations require the strict adherence to a musical score, the distinction between admissible and inadmissible is sharp. But where one holds that the score may be arguably overridden for good reasons, then the distinction between admissible and inadmissible interpretations becomes as gradual as the nature of those reasons will allow. In other words, the multiplist could—but need not—take strict adherence to the score as a criterion for separating admissible from inadmissible interpretations. And then he or she should not take that criterion as the grounds for rationally preferring one or another of the admissible interpretations. Such later judgments would need to be grounded in other considerations, such as musicianship or the like. But we should not commit the musical multiplist to the view that, specifically, strict adherence to the score should separate admissible from inadmissible interpretations. The particular grounds for doing so are open and contestable among multiplists.

Correspondingly, Muti's remark that sometimes it is a *mistake* to interpret a work of music as strictly notated could be construed to mean either that an interpretation which strictly adheres to the score is inadmissible, or that it might be admissible but is not rationally preferred. I embrace the latter rather than the former construal.

In sum, under multiplist conditions it is possible to offer good reasons for one's preferences without at the same time casting those reasons in such strong terms as to implicate an overarching standard. Doing so would oppose the multiplist condition to start with.

Pluralizing Objects-of-Interpretation

Let us proceed to issues concerning the commonality of objects-of-interpretation. For both the singularist and the multiplist there is one

SINGULARISM AND MULTIPLISM

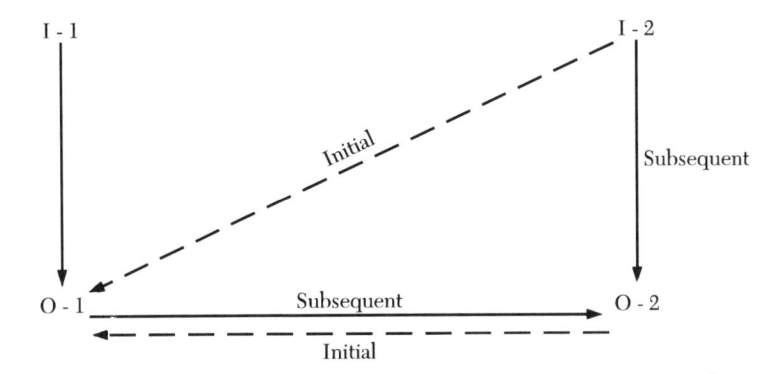

```
I-1                                I-2
|        Initial                    |
|           ─ ─ ─ ─ ─ ─ ─ ─ ─       |
|                                   | Subsequent
|                                   |
↓        Subsequent                 ↓
O-1  ──────────────────────────→  O-2
     ←─ ─ ─ ─ ─ ─ ─ ─ ─ ─ ─ ─
              Initial
```

Object-of-interpretation 1 is pluralized into objects-of-interpretation 1 and 2.

Pluralizing objects-of-interpretation: From a condition initially construed as multiplist, a separate object-of-interpretation is pluralized or bifurcated, and it then answers to the second interpretation. This pluralizing maneuver results in a singularist ideal.

Illustration 4. Pluralizing objects-of-interpretation

object-of-interpretation to which the pertinent interpretations address themselves. When faced with incongruent interpretations of one object-of-interpretation, a singularist might wish to invoke a pluralizing maneuver whereby the one object-of-interpretation is bifurcated into two or more. This maneuver would result in the singularist's ideal of a one-one correspondence between interpretation and object-of-interpretation. Since the two or more interpretations would no longer address the same thing, the initial multiplism and any incongruence between contending interpretations would be eliminated. We may see this bifurcation in Figure 4.

In the history of science, such a pluralizing maneuver is found in the treatment of Goethe's color theory, which was originally thought to compete with Newton's optics as an explanation of light per se. But these theories came to be understood as addressing themselves to different things. While Newton's theory was found to be about the physical properties of light, Goethe's theory was found to be about the phenomenology of perception. Here pluralizing the object-of-interpretation was most fruitful.[14]

In music, Mahler's Symphony No. 6 provides an interesting case

---

14. Stephen Toulmin, *Human Understanding*, vol. 1 (Princeton: Princeton University Press, 1972).

where the pluralizing maneuver might be deployed. According to the original version, the last movement contains three "hammerstrokes" each of which Mahler took to represent tragic episodes in his own life. The last hammerstroke was to have foretold his own death. After conducting the original version in near hysteria, Mahler substituted a second version without the last hammerstroke.[15] No doubt the drama of the first version is lacking in the second. Now, were the pluralizing maneuver to be deployed, the first and second versions would be taken as constituting different objects-of-interpretation, so contending interpretations of each would not, strictly speaking, compete. No multiplism would thereby obtain.

In contrast, it has been charged that Leopold Stokowski's transcription of Bach's Toccata and Fugue is a barbarism of Bach's original object-of-interpretation. This complaint could be answered by deploying the pluralizing maneuver. One might say that Stokowski's is not yet another interpretation of Bach's object-of-interpretation. Rather, it is of another object-of-interpretation altogether. The deployment of the pluralizing maneuver here would be at least contentious.

In turn, in Chapter 3 I shall discuss interpretations of Vincent Van Gogh's *Potato Eaters*. I shall compare competing and incongruent interpretations of the same object-of-interpretation, and the pluralizing maneuver will be assumed not to be a plausible way of eliminating the incongruities.

Aggregating Objects-of-Interpretation

There is an analogue to the pluralizing maneuver, which we may refer to as the "aggregating maneuver." According to it, what initially appear to be more than one distinct object-of-interpretation are aggregated or collected into a common object-of-interpretation, which may then answer to one or more competing interpretations.

Drawing from the above examples, one would deploy the aggregating maneuver in order to argue that Newton's and Goethe's objects-of-interpretation really are one after all; that the two versions

---

15. Norman Del Mar, *Mahler's Sixth Symphony: A Study* (London: Eulenberg Books, 1980).

SINGULARISM AND MULTIPLISM

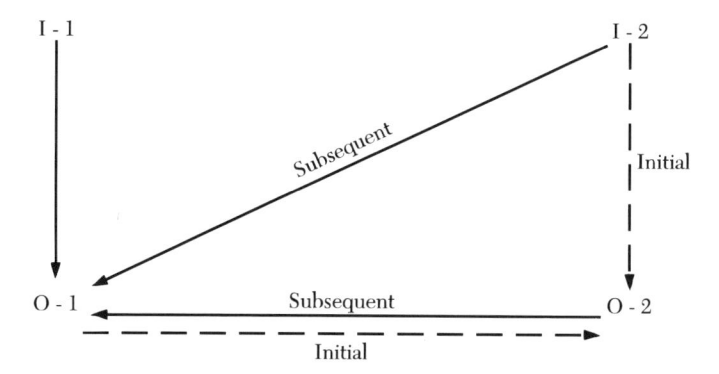

```
I-1                                    I-2
 |                                      |
 |         Subsequent                   |
 |                                      | Initial
 |                                      |
 |                                      |
 ▼                                      ▼
O-1  ◄──────── Subsequent ──────── O-2
     ─ ─ ─ ─ ─ ─ ─ ─ ─ ─ ─ ─ ─ ─ ─ ▶
                Initial
```

Objects-of-interpretation 1 and 2 aggregated into object-of-interpretation 1.

Aggregating objects-of-interpretation: From a condition construed initially as singularist—where different interpretations address different objects-of-interpretation—the separate objects-of-interpretation are aggregated into a common object-of-interpretation which then answers to two or more interpretations. This aggregating maneuver results in a multiplist condition.

Illustration 5. Aggregating objects-of-interpretation

of Mahler's Sixth Symphony really are interpretations of one object-of-interpretation; that Stokowski's transcription really is an interpretation of Bach's self-same Toccata and Fugue; that what will be seen to be different interpretations of Van Gogh's *Potato Eaters* really are interpretations of one object-of-interpretation. Just as there are no general algorithmic rules about the appropriateness of invoking the pluralizing maneuver, there are no such rules about the appropriateness of invoking the aggregating maneuver. Such judgments should be made on a piecemeal basis.

Pluralizing and Aggregating Interpretations

These maneuvers have been concerned with pluralizing or aggregating objects-of-interpretation. Analogous moves are available with respect to interpretations themselves. For example, the multiplist confronting a single interpretation of an object-of-interpretation may seek to affect a multiplist condition by pluralizing the single interpretation. A Marxist-feminist interpretation of Van Gogh's object-of-interpretation may be pluralized into two interpretations: one Marxist, the other feminist. This maneuver is shown schematically in Illustration 6.

```
            Subsequent
I - 1 ◄──────────────────► I - 2
      ─ ─ ─ ─ ─ ─ ─ ─ ─
            Initial

                    Subsequent

                 O - 1
```

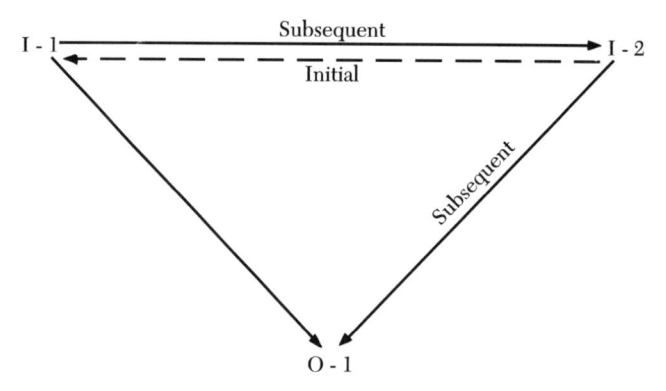

Pluralizing Interpretations: Interpretation-1 is pluralized into Interpretations-1 and 2. From a condition initially construed as singularist, a separate interpretation is pluralized, resulting in a multiplist condition.

Illustration 6. Pluralizing interpretations

Correspondingly, where the singularist confronts a multiplicity of interpretations of a common object-of-interpretation he or she may aggregate interpretations to effect a singularist condition. A Marxist and a feminist interpretation of Van Gogh's object-of-interpretation may be aggregated into a single Marxist-feminist interpretation. This maneuver is shown in Illustration 7.

Clearly, identity conditions of objects-of-interpretation or of interpretations themselves must be in place in order to say whether, in

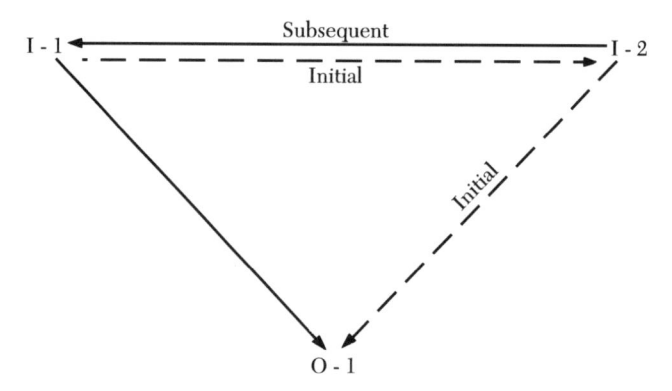

```
            Subsequent
I - 1 ◄──────────────────► I - 2
      ─ ─ ─ ─ ─ ─ ─ ─ ─
            Initial

                    Initial

                 O - 1
```

Aggregating Interpretations: Interpretations 1 and 2 are aggregated into Interpretation 1. From a condition initially construed as multiplist, separate interpretations are aggregated, resulting in a singularist condition.

Illustration 7. Aggregating interpretations

particular cases, the pluralizing or aggregating of objects-of-interpretation (as in Illustrations 4 or 5) or the pluralizing or aggregating of interpretations themselves (as in Illustrations 6 or 7) is warranted. Here too, such conditions cannot be articulated in a general algorithmic way independently of the context of pertinent examples. For example, a Marxist-feminist interpretation of Van Gogh's *Potato Eaters* may well count as one when it opposes, say, a liberal interpretation. Under other circumstances, for example, where Marxists and feminists debate among themselves, the initial Marxist-feminist interpretation—taken initially as one—might well be pluralized into two distinct interpretations.

Pluralizing and Aggregating the Aims of Interpretation

In my discussion of the separability of grounds for admissibility versus grounds for preferability between admissible interpretations, I have assumed that admissibility is to be understood as admissibility with respect to a given aim of interpretation. That is, the discussion whether or not a given object-of-interpretation answers to a single or to several interpretations has been pursued on the assumption that a given aim of interpretation is held constant. For example, in the musical case, one's aim may be to render public as authentic a performance as possible and no more. Yet another interpreter may aim to perform a work in as dramatic a manner as possible, and these aims may or may not converge. Where there are several, perhaps nonconverging, aims, then the multiplism in question is compounded if, that is, there is no overarching standard in virtue of which those aims may be conclusively adjudicated.

Where nonconverging aims of interpretation are in play, the claim that the grounds for admissibility should be distinct from grounds for preferability would need to be adjusted accordingly. That is, one could imagine a situation in which, with respect to one interpretive aim, certain grounds for separating admissible interpretations from inadmissible interpretations are kept distinct from the grounds for preferring one of a number of admissible interpretations. But with respect to another interpretive aim, what might have functioned as a ground for separating admissible interpretations from inadmissible interpretations in the first case might well be grounds for preferences in the second case. If one were to assume that absolute fidelity to the score was a condition for admissibility, one ground for preferring one interpretation over another admissible interpretation might be, as I say, its dramatic effect. But if one were to adopt dramatic effect as a ground for admissibility, then it could not be used as a ground for preferring one admissible interpretation over another admissible interpretation. In such a context, other considerations, such as elegance, perhaps, might be introduced. The general point is that with respect to a given interpretive aim, pertinent grounds must be kept distinct. And, when several nonconverging aims are in play, those grounds concerned with admissibility (versus inadmissibility) or, alternatively, those grounds concerned with preferability (amongst admissible interpretations) may be mixed and matched.

Now, when faced with a putatively multiplist case a singularist might seek to install a singularist condition by indicating that the interpretations initially deemed admissible actually answer to different aims. In such a case, singularism would be restored in a way rather parallel to the case where an object-of-interpretation is pluralized to transform a putatively multiplist case to a singularist one. Here too the reasonableness of aggregating of pluralizing aims would have to be judged on a piecemeal basis.

Multiplism as Relativism

Let us consider whether multiplism is a kind of relativism, and if so, whether it is vulnerable to certain objections to relativism. We may broadly characterize relativism as holding that cognitive, moral, or aesthetic claims—involving such values as truth, meaningfulness, rightness, reasonableness, appropriateness, aptness, or the like—are relative to the contexts in which they appear. And the range of such contexts may extend from a highly localized person-specific or occasion-specific state to that of a community, culture, tradition, historical epoch, or the like. Relativism denies the viability of grounding the pertinent claims in ahistorical, acultural, or absolutist terms.

Relativism is often motivated by the recognition of cultural or historical diversity, but that recognition cannot be equated with relativism. Cultural or historical diversity is logically compatible with either relativism or antirelativism. Although claims of such diversities often appear in accounts of why and how certain standards of evaluation do not apply, relativism is not thereby necessitated. The invitation that one ought to seek or develop further standards remains open.

Of course, to be a relativist at very general levels is not to accede to an extreme relativism, which holds that each belief is as good as another. On this extreme view each belief should be judged according to the unique circumstances of its appearance. This extreme view is absurd because, at least, the claim of uniqueness here carries with it an unwarranted implication of incomparability. But other forms of relativism ought not be dismissed on these grounds. Even if one concedes relativism at general levels, extreme relativism is not necessitated.

Where standards of evaluation give out at the bounds of designated contexts, relativists might expand the horizon of their inquiry. A disciplinary matrix may be placed within an ever-wider cultural matrix; a cultural matrix may be placed within a cross-cultural matrix; these in turn may be placed within an historical matrix or a species-specific matrix; and so on. The end of inquiry may be indefinitely deferred.[16] Where the standards in such designated contexts give out altogether, relativists characteristically remain silent. And such silence may derive from the belief that here the search for pertinent standards makes no sense. It might be urged that standards are formulable only internal to designated contexts. Where they give out, standards give out. Here the controversy between relativists and antirelativists is seen in its starkest form.

Characteristically the contexts in relativism are formulated in terms of conceptual schemes. Along antirelativist and antirealist lines, Donald Davidson argues that the very idea of a conceptual scheme (or a conceptual framework) is incoherent.[17] His view, if right, undercuts any relativism which is so formulated as to claim that pertinent values are relative to conceptual schemes, or to their cognates. Now, insofar as the range of ideally admissible interpretations is formulated in terms of practices, it might be held that practices function as conceptual

---

16. For an interesting discussion of this issue see Ben-Ami Scharfstein, *The Dilemma of Context* (New York: New York University Press, 1989).

17. Donald Davidson, "On the Very Idea of a Conceptual Scheme," in Michael Krausz and Jack Meiland, eds., *Relativism: Cognitive and Moral* (Notre Dame: Notre Dame University Press, 1982).

schemes for singularism and multiplism. The threat is that both singularism and multiplism might be incoherent on this account.

Davidson argues, roughly, that the coherence of the idea of a conceptual scheme requires the coherence of the idea of an alternative conceptual scheme. But this idea is incoherent too. If an alternative conceptual scheme is translatable into the first scheme, it is not "alternative." And if it is not thus translatable, nothing intelligible can be said about it to distinguish it from the first conceptual scheme. Since grounds for distinguishing a conceptual scheme from an alternative conceptual scheme do not obtain, the distinction collapses, and with it the coherence of the very idea of a conceptual scheme. And with that, the coherence of those forms of relativism which assume it also collapses.

Davidson's argument is vulnerable to a counterargument of Alasdair MacIntyre.[18] MacIntyre distinguishes between translatability and understanding, and he claims that one can understand two cultures or appropriate portions thereof while not being able to translate between them. Indeed, the bilingual person needs to be able to do this in order to determine—as he or she does—what is translatable from one culture to another. Just as untranslatability does not entail a limit on understanding, understanding does not entail translatability. MacIntyre's argument undercuts Davidson's claim that the coherence of the idea of a conceptual scheme or an alternative conceptual scheme is a matter of translatability. Thus Davidson's argument against the idea of a conceptual scheme fails. Correspondingly, the idea of a practice, understood as a cognate of a conceptual scheme, may on these grounds remain coherent. In any event, an argument would need to be mounted to the effect that practices are cognates of conceptual schemes in order to make practices vulnerable to Davidson's argument.

Nonconverging Interpretations: An Alternate View

The present account is generally sympathetic with that of Joseph Margolis who capitalizes on the possibility that nonconverging inter-

---

18. Alasdair MacIntyre, "Relativism, Power, and Philosophy," in Michael Krausz, ed., *Relativism: Interpretation and Confrontation* (Notre Dame: Notre Dame University Press, 1989).

pretations can be legitimately defended, not as an interim or tolerable condition approaching an ideal condition of full convergence, but rather as a condition that is itself ideally admissible. Margolis holds that this condition reflects the very nature of cultural entities and their interpretations. It will be instructive to indicate the areas of agreement and disagreement with his account.

Margolis dissociates himself from the view of E. D. Hirsch, for example, that it is the individual author's intentions that should be the criterion for the single right interpretation. At the same time, he dissociates himself from Beardsley's account of the internal autonomy of the work in relation to which one should fix upon singular meaning. Rather, along Wittgensteinian lines, he maintains that what is internal or external to a cultural entity is historically open. Such openness is not due to an epistemic lack. Rather, what is internal or external is essentially unstable. The meaning of a cultural entity is imputed, yet constrained by the social contexts in which it appears.

We might comment here that the very intelligibility of an individual creator's intentions is a function of the intelligibility of the cultural context in which he or she works and lives. To understand the kind of thing that painter Anselm Kiefer does, for example, involves understanding quite a lot about postwar German consciousness. The intelligibility of his work does not depend upon his intentions construed independently of "social intentionality." Individual intentionality is empty without social intentionality.

Margolis holds that one should be as inclusionary as possible about ideally admissible interpretations of cultural entities. While he does not countenance contradictory pairs of interpretations, he holds that characteristically bipolar values are inappropriately applied to interpretations of cultural entities. Rather, he invokes values other than truth (understood in a bipolar way) including plausibility, reasonableness, aptness, appropriateness, and the like. These values are not to be understood as stand-ins for bipolar truth or falsity. Margolis holds that there is no reductive strategy in virtue of which plausibility-type values are reducible to truth or falsity. Given this caveat, he tolerates competition between so-called incongruent but not logically contradictory interpretations. The clash in the assertion of incongruent interpretations would be weaker than the clash in the assertion of contradictory interpretations.

Margolis says:

> Thus, musical interpretations A and B of Brahms's *Fourth Symphony* or literary interpretations A and B of *Hamlet* are incompatible in the straightforward sense that there is no interpretation C in which A and B can be combined. But that is not to say that A and B cannot both be plausible. (The equivocation on "A" and "B" is benign enough.) When, therefore, I say that "we allow seemingly incompatible accounts of a given work to stand as confirmed," I mean to draw attention . . . to the fact that the accounts in question would be incompatible construed in terms of a model of truth and falsity, but *not* incompatible construed in terms of plausibility.[19]

Now, Margolis groups appropriateness and aptness along with other such values as plausibility and probability. This grouping is unfortunate, since the latter notions are elliptical for "plausible with respect to truth" or "probable with respect to truth." At the same time, aptness and appropriateness do not suggest such a reading. To say that such-and-such an interpretation is appropriate or apt need not invite saying that it is so with respect to truth.

But having distinguished values that are elliptical for some cognate of truth and those that are not—leaving open whether some nonbipolar construal of truth will go through in the end—it would still seem that one could not hold both that A was more apt than B and that B was more apt than A on a given standard of aptness. Of course, pertinent standards may be incommensurable, but then "aptness" would be equivocal. So, even aptness and appropriateness may exhibit the exclusivity or bipolarity which Margolis resists. It is one thing to concede—as I do—that standards may be incommensurable. It is another thing to hold—as Margolis does—that, with respect to a given standard, judgments of A over B or B over A are nonexclusive.

Alternatively, we may offer an account consistent with Margolis's motivation to preserve both claims that A is better than B and that B is better than A, which involves a multiplicity of standards that are themselves not in turn subsumable under a univocal overarching standard. That is, drawing upon familiar features of incommensurability, one might construe incongruence as a case in which, for a given object-of-interpretation, there may be in play a number of standards that

---

19. Margolis, *Art and Philosophy*, p. 164.

resist being subsumed under and ranked according to an overarching univocal standard. Because the standards would be incongruent, the pertinent interpretations would be incongruent.

Such would be the case for the example of the first movement of Beethoven's First Symphony. There, the standards of "faithfulness to the score" and "aesthetic consistency" are incongruent, and there is no available overarching univocal standard which could rank those standards in turn. Yet, proponents of each interpretation may argue for the aptness or appropriateness of his or her interpretation. Each may provide good though inconclusive reasons for his or her interpretation. With respect to each standard in turn, interpretation A is better than B, or B is better than A. When allowing the admissibility of incongruent interpretations, one should unpack the notion of incongruity along the lines of the incongruity of the pertinent standards. In short, we do not need to understand the admissibility of nonconverging interpretations in terms of values that are not bipolar. Incommensurability is enough.

I shall return to this issue in Chapter 4. But now it is time to turn directly to the very idea of an interpretation.

3

Imputational Interpretation in Art, Poetry, Persons, and Cultures

The idea of interpretation resists strict or algorithmic rules about correct application. As Stuart Hampshire has remarked, interpretation is not a distinct concept, so our starting point must be the typical circumstances in which the word is put to use.[1] Hilary Putnam reinforces the point when he says: "We all realize that we cannot hope to mechanize interpretation. The dream of formalizing interpretation is as utopian as the dream of formalizing nonparadigmatic rationality itself. Not only is interpretation a highly informal activity, guided by few, if any, settled rules or methods, but it is one that involves much more than linear propositional reasoning. It involves our imagination, our feelings—in short, our full sensibility."[2]

Imputational Interpretation

In Chapter 1, I argued for multiplism from the multiplicity of interpretive practices. There is a separate argument for multiplism which

---

1. Stuart Hampshire, "Types of Interpretation," in Sidney Hook, ed., *Art and Philosophy* (New York: New York University Press, 1966), pp. 101–2.
2. Hilary Putnam, *Realism with a Human Face* (Cambridge: Harvard University Press, 1992), p. 129.

derives from the imputation or the constitution of objects-of-interpretation by interpretation. Although I favor this argument, we should recognize that the thesis of multiplism does not require it. According to the imputationalist view, an interpretation may constitute or impute features of its object-of-interpretation. "Imputation" here is not to be taken in a motivational sense—as in imputing a motive—but in its constitutive sense. In turn, imputational interpretation should be contrasted with "nonimputational" interpretation in which the character of the object-of-interpretation is understood to be fully autonomous or independent of interpretation as such.

Joseph Margolis puts the "imputationalist" view broadly: "'Interpreting'... suggests a touch of virtuosity, an element of performance, a shift from a stable object whose properties are enumerable to an object whose properties pose something of a puzzle or challenge—with emphasis... on some inventive use of materials present, on the added contribution of the interpreter, and on a certain openness toward possible alternative interpretations"[3]

Imputational interpretation involves imputing properties which, in being imputed, actually become intrinsically part of the work. As Margolis says, "There is no reason why, granting that criticism proceeds in an orderly way, practices cannot be sustained in which aesthetic designs are rigorously *imputed* to particular works when they cannot be determinately *found* in them."[4]

This chapter will be given over to exemplifying imputational interpretation in various areas in the cultural realm, including face-vase figures; Van Gogh's *Potato Eaters;* Wordsworth's Lucy poem; self-understanding; and other cultures. I shall also introduce related issues as they arise, such as questions concerning the comparison and weighing of competing interpretations. These will be considered more fully in Chapter 4 where the impuionalist view will be discussed in light of possible anti-imputationalist criticisms.

First, consider the face-vase figures below. If one views the central portion as positive space, Figure I may be seen as a vase. Or, viewing the central portion as a negative space, one may see Figure I as a

---

3. Joseph Margolis, *Art and Philosophy* (Atlantic Highlands, N.J.: Humanities Press, 1980), p. 111.
4. Ibid., p. 160.

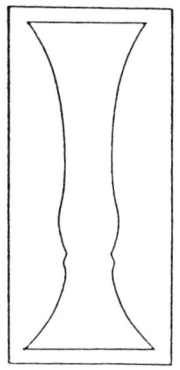

68   INTERPRETATION IN CULTURAL PRACTICES

FIGURE I   FIGURE II
Illustration 8

pair of faces. When interpreting Figures I or II as a vase or as a pair of faces one assigns salience to certain aspects of the figures. When interpreting Figure I as a pair of faces, for example, one assigns salience to the sharp corners where the foreheads separate the eyes, where the noses join the mouths, and so forth. Seen otherwise, these features would be interpreted as angular contours of a vase. Similarly, when Figure II is interpreted as a pair of faces (though doing so would be forced), the elongated upper contours would have been assigned salience so as to interpret them as foreheads. In this case the aspects would have been imputed in different ways. Here the interpretation—face or vase—prompts one to impute salience to certain features of the presented configuration, which in turn confirms the propriety of interpreting the configuration as a face or a vase.

Generally, in imputational interpretation what is taken as the object-of-interpretation is partly a function of the interpretation under consideration. And, as in the present case, whether we accept one interpretation over another is not so much a matter of the fit between an interpretation and an autonomous or practice-independent object-of-interpretation, but is rather a matter of the fit between an interpretation and the object-of-interpretation *construed in the light of the interpretation in question*. Here the object-of-interpretation is understood in terms of its imputed properties. As in Figure II, we accept the vase interpretation over the face interpretation largely because seeing the upper contours of the configuration as a pair of elongated foreheads is more forced than seeing it as an elegant opening of a vase. Seeing the contour as a vase is less forced or more perspicuous than seeing the contour as a pair of faces. When the face and vase interpretations are being compared, the contours are seen as faces and vase respectively. The interpretations and their objects-of-interpretation are taken as packages. It is the packages that are being compared. Thus, to say that we accept one interpretation over another is to say that we accept one package over another, and in so doing we do not hold fixed an object-of-interpretation independent of interpretation as such. This feature of imputational interpretation will be exemplified in the examples that follow.

Notice that when we interpret Figure II more perspicuously as a vase rather than a pair of faces, the affirmation that this interpretation is "more appropriate" or "more reasonable" does not render inappropriate or unreasonable or inapt the alternative interpretation. And this concession does not depend upon the absence of enough information at hand to show that one interpretation is conclusively inappropriate or unreasonable or inapt. No fuller accounting of the psychological or historical context in which Figures I or II are interpreted would provide the grounds for conclusively unseating one of the interpretations.

But one might suggest that this really is a case of visual ambiguity and that visual ambiguity need not involve imputing an object-of-interpretation. Further, it might be urged, even though an image (or, by extension a text) may be ambiguous when taken out of context, it does not follow that there is no code or system of rules of interpretation that could disambiguate it.

But in this example there is no single context that, if uncovered, would singularly disambiguate. For each of the interpretations a context could be postulated that might make it appropriate to some degree. Yet there is no overarching standard in virtue of which one could say that one interpretation, with its postulated context, is conclusively better than another. This is why no fuller accounting of the psychological or historical context in which the figures are interpreted could provide the grounds for conclusively unseating all but one of the interpretations.

One might reply that there must be some constraints on what can be plausibly imputed. Not just anything one can interpret a thing *as* will constitute an appropriate imputation. But from the thesis of imputational interpretation it does not follow that anything one imputes is admissible, for there are constraints in each case. Given our common visual codes, it would be inadmissible to interpret either of the face-vase figures, for example, as Venus de Milo. None of their elements correspond to Venus de Milo. While there are no general criteria for separating admissible from inadmissible interpretations, there are general considerations—such as sufficient correspondence—which pertain to appropriate local constraints. And they implicate socially intentional contexts, such as common visual codes. Such contexts characteristically do not conclusively issue in a single right imputation or interpretation.

Consider imputation in various interpretations of Vincent Van Gogh's *Potato Eaters*.[5] This painting has been the subject of numerous incongruous types of interpretation, including formalist, psychological, Marxist, and feminist. Each interpretation imputes salience to different features. Consider first a formalist interpretation, which takes as salient aspects of the painting that pertain to what formalists characterize as "significant form."[6] Formalist interpretations characteristically concern themselves with features "internal" to the object-of-interpretation. Assuming a strict distinction between what is internal and external to an object-of-interpretation, the formalist seeks to restrict interpretation to "internal" elements. The formalist holds that those who address "external" aspects are offering interpretations of historical, social, or psychological conditions that merely surround the object-of-interpretation. They do not, strictly speaking, address the object-of-interpretation proper. Yet because the distinction between internal and external cannot be sharply drawn, we shall see that in practice formalists inevitably implicate features "external" to the object-of-interpretation as well.

H. P. Bremmer, for example, offers what he characterizes as a formalist interpretation of the *Potato Eaters* which emphasizes the

---

5. I am indebted to my former student Rebekah Brock who worked on this example with me.
6. See Jaqueline V. Falkenheim, *Roger Fry and the Beginnings of Formalist Art Criticism* (Ann Arbor: UMI Research Press, 1980). See also Bernard Harrison, *Form and Content* (Oxford: Basil Blackwell, 1973) on the distinction between form and content.

Illustration 9. Van Gogh, *The Potato Eaters*. Courtesy of the Vincent Van Gogh Foundation/Van Gogh Museum, Amsterdam.

formal parallels between the mugs and the family, but, we should note, the "internal" is not easily contained.

> A table is placed in the middle of the scene; it is stoutly made, but shows traces of abraded edges... here he [Van Gogh] apparently wishes to reveal something more than the poetry of such an interior—how this all grimly reflects an image of life's hardness. One senses this also in the mugs which are being filled by the woman on the right. One feels here that more is expressed than the mere fact of four mugs—that their placement so closely together fits in with the total action depicted in the painting and reflects the same idea of interrelated unity that one associates with the family itself.[7]

We need not be too concerned that Bremmer's is not a strictly formalist interpretation, since one may not be able to offer a strictly formalist example at all. As Ludwig Wittgenstein suggested and as Morris Weitz elaborated, the very distinction between internal and external cannot be sustained.[8] But for our more limited purposes we should note that when Bremmer resists intentional features of the depicted figures and remarks about the formal parallel between the closely placed mugs and the unity of the family, he assigns salience to those features. As such he imputes an object-of-interpretation about which his interpretation speaks. In so doing he secures his broadly formalist interpretation.

In contrast, consider a broadly psychological (or psychological-psychoanalytic) interpretation. H. R. Graetz[9] interprets *The Potato Eaters* in terms of the inner conflicts in Van Gogh's life, drawing heavily upon Van Gogh's correspondence with his brother Theo. In

---

7. H. P. Bremmer, "Introductory Appreciations," in Bogomila Welsh-Ovcharov, ed., *Van Gogh in Perspective* (Englewood Cliffs, N.J.: Prentice Hall, 1974), p. 85.

8. Morris Weitz, "The Role of Theory in Aesthetics," *Journal of Aesthetics and Art Criticism* 15 (1956), 27–35.

9. H. R. Graetz, *The Symbolic Language of Vincent Van Gogh* (New York: McGraw Hill, 1963). Ronald Dworkin's method of expanding the evidential base could be here exemplified. Faced with the challenge of eliminating a multiplicity of contending interpretations, one might be tempted to expand the context of the inquiry to include considerations (in this case) from biography or social history, and so forth.

noting that the depicted figures do not look at each other, Graetz sees them as lonely and isolated. The two men are turned toward the elder woman, but she is looking downward. She is further detached because a wall in the background is between her and the old man beside her. Graetz notes the sad expression of the younger man and locates the name "Vincent" darkly painted (and imperceptible in most reproductions) on his chair. And, the darkness and detachment of the figures express a lack of love and understanding which Vincent felt in his parents' house. He longed for "a ray of light, or kindness" represented by the lantern. At the same time, the lamp "throws equal light on everyone in the room and brings out the warming effect of the steam from the hot potatoes and coffee."[10] Graetz holds that this light is a symbol of love for Vincent.

Graetz's interpretation takes the painting as a basis for interpreting Van Gogh's psychological state. The imagery of the painting is treated as evidence for a psychological hypothesis about Van Gogh. But the matter does not end here. For it is in virtue of that hypothesis that Graetz turns back to the painting to impute or assign salience to certain of its aspects. Here we see how the interpretation imputes an object-of-interpretation, how it certifies a way in which what is to be interpreted is constituted.

Consider yet another psychological interpretation of the painting. Albert Lubin agrees with Graetz about the psychological importance of the light. "To Vincent, the glowing lights of a house spoke of warmth and happiness within." But Lubin goes farther than Graetz to suggest that the light in this painting is connected with Van Gogh's preoccupation with lights of the sky. "Stars twinkling in the sky revealed the acceptance of the dead in heaven."[11] Lubin connects this point to the faceless and unearthly child in the foreground. The steam rising from the food—out of sight of the viewer—creates a heavenly air about the figure's head and shoulders. Lubin takes it that this child figure represents Vincent's dead brother who was born and died exactly one year before his own birth, and who had the same name.

10. Graetz, *The Symbolic Language of Vincent Van Gogh*, p. 34.
11. Albert Lubin, *Stranger on the Earth: A Psychological Biography of Vincent Van Gogh* (New York: Holt, Rinehart, and Winston, 1972, pp. 19–20.

Lubin hypothesizes that the knowledge of his dead brother, whose grave was around the corner from Van Gogh's home in his youth, must have had a profound effect on him.

Thus, for Lubin, the painting is about mourning. "It would seem that Vincent was portraying the grieving mother who could not mother him; her spirit remained with the dead but perfect child who stood between them, separating them in the painting as in life."[12] And, he remarks: "His brother's example taught Vincent that being dead meant being loved and cherished, while being alive meant being rejected."[13]

Lubin justifies assigning salience to the mother, the child, and the Vincent of the painting by noting that in Van Gogh's preparatory sketches only those three figures appeared. The other figures, added to later sketches, are thought by Lubin to be his father (who Vincent felt sided with his mother) and his sister Wilhelmina (who was often on his side).[14]

Despite the differences in their imputing interpretations, the resulting objects-of-interpretation of Bremmer (on the one hand) and Graetz and Lubin (on the other hand) are sufficiently similar for the three interpretations to compete. Of course, were one to pluralize the object-of-interpretation—that is, argue that each interpretation is really about another object-of-interpretation, whatever their relation to the physical canvas—the interpretations could not compete. But it seems perfectly natural to say that the formalist and the psychological interpretations do address an object-of-interpretation sufficiently common for the interpretations to compete.

We have considered one formalist interpretation and two psychological interpretations. Let us turn to a Marxist-feminist interpretation. For example, Griselda Pollock states that her concern "is to reconstruct the circumstances of the production of one of the major projects of Van Gogh's programme as a painter of peasants."[15]

Identifying Van Gogh as a person of the upper-middle class, Pollock

---

12. Ibid., p. 100.
13. Ibid., p. 83.
14. Ibid., pp. 100–101.
15. Griselda Pollock, "Van Gogh and the Poor Slaves: Images of Rural Labor as Modern Art," *Art History* 11 (September 1988), 406.

understands Van Gogh's preparatory studies of hands, faces, and gestures as explorations of "otherness." Drawing upon Van Gogh's letters, Pollock underscores Van Gogh's awareness of and opposition to the plight of the peasants he so often depicted. Further, Pollock argues that Van Gogh "savages the conventions within which peasant women were fashioned for salon viewing." These women are no longer portrayed as innocent "natural" woman of the country as opposed to tarnished working woman of the city. Rather, they are full of physical peculiarities. Their depiction is no longer part of the tradition of the "pleasantness of viewing peasants." For Pollock, the painting is about manual labor. It is about otherness and difference. It addresses itself to the bourgeoisie and creates a "synaesthetic effect of the actual feel, smell and look of primitive faces. Their faces, their hands and even the way they sit are different."[16]

About her general approach, Pollock says "This article attempts to analyze the conditions of existence and reception of a particular painting. This involves locating the painting within a semantic field into which this particular text entered and on which its meaning (or failure to achieve meaning) depended historically.... [This procedure diminishes] the centrality of the artist as originating individual by focusing on the social and the historical circumstance in which productive activities take place."[17]

This interpretation may be given extra weight in light of Van Gogh's construal of his own work. Yet, we should caution that for reasons of projection, self-deception, and the like, his remarks cannot be taken as conclusive on these matters. Still, from Van Gogh's considerable correspondence we may well consider his own words.

> I have tried to make it clear how these people, eating their potatoes under the lamplight, have dug the earth with those very hands they put in the dish, and so it speaks of manual labor, and how they have honestly earned their food. I have wanted to give the impression of quite a different way of living than that of us civilized people. Therefore I am not at all anxious for everyone to like it or to admire it at once.... It would be wrong, I think, to give a peasant picture

16. Ibid., pp. 419, 420, 428.
17. Ibid., pp. 406–9.

a certain conventional smoothness. If a peasant picture smells of bacon, smoke, potato-steam, all right, that's not unhealthy; if a stable smells of dung, all right, that belongs to a stable; if the field has an odor of ripe corn or potatoes or of manure, that's healthy especially for people from the city. Such pictures may teach them something.

I should be desperate if my figures were correct. You must know that I do not want them to be academically correct.... My great longing is to learn to make these incorrectnesses, these deviations, remodelling, changes of reality that they may become, yes, untruth if you like—but more true than the literal truth.[18]

As in the case of Graetz's and Lubin's psychological interpretations, Pollock's Marxist-feminist interpretation addresses an object-of-interpretation in a wider context. Again we confront the question whether these interpretations address themselves to a sufficiently common object-of-interpretation. For example, consider the gaze of the male figure on the far left of the painting. Bremmer does not assign salience to the gaze as such, but sees it as part of "the whole figure in concentrating on the business of eating."[19] His interpretation differs from those of Graetz, Lubin, and Pollock, all of whom assign salience to the gaze, though in different ways. Graetz interprets the gazes of all of the figures in terms of loneliness and isolation. He notes the "mute appeal" of this particular figure which is ignored by the matriarchal figure. Although the gaze is directed at the older woman, it "goes beyond her into infinity."[20] In contrast, Lubin sees the gaze as intended for the mother figure and precisely not passing on into infinity. He interprets the gaze as revealing Van Gogh's desire for love and interaction with his mother. Van Gogh's need for a caring and sympathetic mother causes him to reach out longingly for his mourning mother. For Lubin, this gaze is an attempt to make contact and to invite the love that Van Gogh so desired. Pollock also sees the

18. Letters of Vincent Van Gogh, in J. G. Van Gelder, "The Potato Eaters," in Welsh-Ovcharov, *Van Gogh in Perspective*, nos. 404, 418.
19. H. P. Bremmer, "Introductory Appreciations," in Welsh-Ovcharov, *Van Gogh in Perspective*, p. 84.
20. Graetz, *The Symbolic Language of Vincent Van Gogh*, p. 34.

ART, POETRY, PERSONS, AND CULTURES 77

figures as lonely and isolated. But she sees an attempt at interaction only in the gazes of the elderly couple on the far right. Pollock interprets the gaze of the elder man next to the matriarchal figure as a gaze of gratitude for the filling of his cup or in anticipation that it is about to be filled.[21]

Generally, then, what is taken as salient is in keeping with the interpretations favored: Bremmer's disvaluing the intentionality of the figures; Graetz's and Lubin's valuing individual intentionality in terms of the satisfaction of Van Gogh's emotional needs and desires; and Pollock's valuing of the social intentionality embodied in the drink received, for example. For these various interpretations to compete they must address themselves to an object-of-interpretation that is sufficiently common between them. Again, while it is natural to regard them as addressing a sufficiently common object-of-interpretation, one can well imagine a plausible case being made that such commonality does not obtain—for example that Lubin's psychological interpretation is just using *The Potato Eaters* to compose Van Gogh's psychological biography.

Analogously, one might question the identity of the interpretation in question. For example, one might be tempted to tease out the feminist from the Marxist strains in Pollock's Marxist-feminist interpretation, and suggest by such a pluralizing of interpretation that whatever other grounds for multiplism there might be, such a maneuver would multiply it in turn. There seems no ready algorithm to settle such questions. Such issues of identity would need to be pursued in the context of more textured discussions in which the relations between competing interpretations would be unpacked.

Let us consider a third case of imputational interpretation, this time from literature. E. D. Hirsch provides the example, although he does so for very different purposes.[22] It is that of Wordsworth's Lucy Poem,

---

21. Pollock, "Van Gogh and the Poor Slaves," 423.
22. E. D. Hirsch, Jr., *Validity in Interpretation* (New Haven: Yale University Press, 1967), pp. 227–28. The passages that Hirsch cites from Brooks and Bateson are drawn from Cleanth Brooks, "Irony as a Principle of Structure," in *Literary Opinion in America*, ed. M. D. Zabel, 2d ed. (New York: Harper, 1951), p. 736; F. W. Bateson, *English Poetry: A Critical Introduction* (London: Longmans, Green, 1950), pp. 33, 80–81.

"A Slumber Did My Spirit Seal," as interpreted first by Cleanth Brooks and alternatively by F. W. Bateson. To start with, here is Wordsworth's poem.

> A slumber did my spirit seal;
>   I had no human fears:
> She seemed a thing that could not feel
>   The touch of earthly years.
>
> No motion has she now, no force;
>   She neither hears nor sees;
> Rolled round in earth's diurnal course,
>   With rocks, and stones, and trees.

And here, taken from Hirsch, are excerpts from the two interpretations of the final lines of the poem. The first is by Cleanth Brooks.

> [Wordsworth] attempts to suggest something of the lover's agonized shock at the loved one's present lack of motion—of his response to her utter and horrible inertness.... Part of the effect, of course, resides in the fact that a dead lifelessness is suggested more sharply by an object's being whirled about by something else than by an image of the object in repose. But there are other matters which are at work here: the sense of the girl's falling back into the clutter of things, companioned by things chained like a tree to one particular spot, or by things completely inanimate like rocks and stones. ... [She] is caught up helplessly into the empty whirl of the earth which measures and makes time. She is touched by and held by earthly time in its most powerful and horrible image.

Here is the second interpretation by Bateson.

> The final impression the poem leaves is not of two contrasting moods, but of a single mood mounting to a climax in the pantheistic magnificence of the last two lines.... The vague living-Lucy of this poem is opposed to the grander dead-Lucy who has become involved in the sublime processes of nature. We put the poem down satisfied, because its last two lines succeed in effecting a reconciliation between the two philosophies or social attitudes. Lucy is

actually more alive now that she is dead, because she is now a part of Nature, and not just a human "thing."

Brooks' and Bateson's interpretations of the poem impute different meanings to the text by taking different aspects as salient. For example, Bateson does not simply discover as a fact independent of interpretation that the poem has a "pantheistic" meaning. Rather, in so reading the poem he imputes to the text a meaning that can be sustained by the text. And this holds as well for Brooks' incongruent interpretation of the poem as dead-lifelessness. The pantheistic poem has different features from the lifelessness poem, but these are sufficiently common to affirm that the interpretations are about "the same" object-of-interpretation. Of course, one could imagine arguing that they are just not talking about the same object-of-interpretation at all. But such a pluralizing of the object-of-interpretation would seem quite forced. Indeed, Brooks and Bateson themselves understand that their respective interpretations are actually competing.

Indeed, both interpretations are underdetermined by the text; the text is consistent with either of the interpretations. So the last two lines of the poem could be interpreted in either Bateson's or Brooks's way. It is not an epistemic lack that brings us to recognize that the text underdetermines its interpretations. According to the thesis of imputational interpretation, these interpretations are consistent with the text, and they also impute meanings to it and thereby partly constitute their object-of-interpretation.

Now, as a singularist, Hirsch himself would press the view that ideally there is only one single right interpretation, which must be grounded in the will of Wordsworth. But I have indicated why such a move will not work. Hirsch's retreat to the creator's individual intentions does not "save" him from multiplism. But we should not conclude that individual intentions are irrelevant in the discussion of admissibility. As in the musical case considered in Chapter 1, they play a significant, if not conclusive, role in such discussions.

Fourth, let us consider imputational interpretation in self-understanding. Charles Taylor, for example, holds that imputational interpretation is characteristically found in the human sciences, although he does not refer to it by this name.

we have to think of man as a self-interpreting animal. He is necessarily so, for there is no such thing as the structure of meanings for him independently of his interpretations of them; for one is woven into the other. But then the text of our interpretation is not that heterogeneous from what is interpreted; for what is interpreted is itself an interpretation; a self-interpretation which is embedded in a stream of action. It is an interpretation of experiential meaning which contributes to the constitution of this meaning. Or, to put it another way: that of which we are trying to find the coherence is itself partly constituted by self-interpretation.[23]

Such self-constitution or self-imputation may be found in what I call a "personal program" in relation to which one interprets one's own creative achievements for oneself. For example, Roman Jakobson has observed that such artists as Casimir Malevich and Wassily Kandinsky made sense of and interpreted their own works in the light of a kind of reconstruction of their own personal programs.[24] Yet a personal program need not be specific to art, but may apply to one's creative achievements and even more broadly to one's life experience.

While executing a particular work, or while considering a new work, creative artists characteristically confronts the question, What shall I do next? In answer they may look at their artistic corpus in narratist terms. They may, in the form of an interpretation, formulate for themselves a rational reconstruction of their own work, indicating what features they would wish to emphasize, those which they mean to be invariant in the corpus's unfolding history. As present interpreters of their past achievements they may come to recognize that there may have been a preoccupation with this theme, that shape, this color, that space, this feeling, that medium, and so on. And these may be genuine discoveries in the sense that such features may not actually have been intended at the time of production. They may in turn come to value or disvalue features of the reconstructed history of their corpus. Correspondingly, they would be able to judge whether

---

23. Charles Taylor, *Philosophy and the Human Sciences: Philosophical Papers*, vol. 2 (Cambridge: Cambridge University Press, 1985), pp. 26–27.
24. In conversation with Roman Jakobson, February 1978. Interestingly, in *The Structure of Scientific Revolutions*, 2d ed. (Chicago: University of Chicago Press, 1970), Thomas Kuhn makes a parallel observation about Dalton. See pp. 139–41.

a proposed next move is reasonable, appropriate, or apt. Such reconstructions may set constraints on what is reasonable, appropriate, or apt, and they may suggest subsequent moves. Those subsequent moves will reflect the reconstruction presumed. Put otherwise, the interpretation creative artists place on their own past achievements—which is to say which features they take to be salient—may well influence their future directions. By imputing more salience to certain features of their past achievements, creative artists shape their objects-of-interpretation. In this way they may constitute or impute their own creative histories. At subsequent stages they may constitute or impute their own creative histories in different ways.

Something like the idea of a personal program is articulated by Karl Popper in the following way:

> [A] model or map ... with our position marked on it, is part of our ordinary consciousness of self. It normally exists in the form of vague dispositions or programmes; but we can focus our attention upon it whenever we wish, whereupon it may become more elaborate and precise. This map or model is one of a great number of conjectural *theories* about the world which we hold and which we almost constantly call to our aid, as we go along and as we develop, specify, and realize, the programme and the time table of the actions in which we are engaged.[25]

A personal program may help to situate oneself to oneself; to make the self intelligible to the self; to help make sense of oneself to oneself; to motivate the self in its unfolding; to provide a strategy for self-understanding; to embody values in terms of which future choices may be guided; to impute and to constitute oneself; to interpret oneself to oneself.

For illustrative purposes, let us compare two opposing personal programs. In the first instance these programs concern creativity in art, but, more generally, they bear on the imputation and interpretation of the self. Specifically, the *product-centered* personal program holds that the creative process leads up to and ends with the pro-

---

25. Karl R. Popper and John Eccles, *The Self and Its Brain* (Berlin: Springer International, 1977), p. 91.

duction of particular objects. Accordingly, the production of a series of works is best understood in terms of a series of discrete creative processes resulting in individual products. This program devalues the idea that the creation of an art object may be an integral part of a yet larger process that constitutes a creative life. On the other hand, the *process-centered* personal program emphasizes the relations between works, and regards creative products as vehicles for the creative life. Here the creative process has less to do with the production of things, and more with the life-process in which they are embedded. Accordingly, the creative life is made so by engaging in creative acts, the products of these acts revealing and constituting something of the creative life of its artist. On this view, there is a movement to the creative life which the artist, through his or her products, punctuates and documents. The creative product is the embodiment of its maker's life-process, as much as the life-process is constituted by the production of creative products.

The differences between these incongruent personal programs may be revealed more fully by considering a reconstructed dialogue between Larry Briskman (whose interventions are introduced by "T") and myself (whose interventions are introduced by "S").[26]

> S: For me, a particular art object is not the terminus of the process; it punctuates and helps constitute a larger ongoing process of the creative life of the artist. The point of the production of things lies in the process, the movement, the journey. The aim of the movement is its quality.

> T: On my view, a given product is the terminating point of the creative process. The point of the process lies in the product it issues. I do not see why we need to talk about any larger process.

> S: But why should an artist *value* making art products? Why should an artist care about the objects if not because the process expands and develops him or her?

26. See Michael Krausz, "A Painter's View of Self-Development and Creativity," *Leonardo* 13 (Spring 1980), 143–45; and Larry Briskman, "Creativity and Self-Development: A Reply to Michael Krausz," *Leonardo* 13 (1980), 323–25.

T: But by what standards could one judge the life-process? Calling something creative suggests that it meets some standards. In my view we can judge the quality of a work by how well it satisfies a problem-situation or by how well it compares with other products which address themselves to similar problem-situations. I don't see how you can talk of standards for your larger creative life-process.

S: We can evaluate creative products in the way you describe. But that does not address artists' need to reconstitute themselves and their involvement in the larger process as it unfolds. Good or bad works affect the nature and direction of the larger life-process. But there are other considerations as well in assessing the value of the larger process. And the standards of the larger process will enter into the assessment of the particular works. The standards of the life process involve those of self-development, for example. But those standards are provided within the process itself. So, I don't think there is a general answer to your question.

T: My notion of creativity is much more down-to-earth than yours. Mine concerns the production of creative products. Yours seems to concern the growth of the creator as well as the creative products.

S: But being concerned with the growth of the creator is not just an additional and separate thing. The creator is affected by his or her products, and vice versa. From the point of view of the creator, one cannot really separate these concerns.

T: Even so, what distinct standards would there be for evaluating your larger life-process?

S: The making of good works will facilitate self-development. Further, the experience of the making will help constitute the very journey of self-development. The production of things is a means of journeying. And the objects stand as markers on the journey. The art object is both the medium and the record of the self-developing experience. The artist is part of the process. Through self-development one becomes more alive; one becomes more engaged at a deeper level. One experiences things more perspicuously.

T: But I don't see how one judges whether one has made progress in one's self-development. And I don't see how that would be reflected in one's work.

S: When an artist commits him or her self to canvas with an image in mind, what results is characteristically somewhat different from the initial intent. Then, in a retrospective way, the artist sees what has been done, and then projects the next step. In this way, he or she discerns the outlines of the traveled and emerging journey. But with that traveling, the artist gets a fuller sense of where the journey is going, and he or she gets a fuller sense of its emerging aim.

It is similar in self-development. We do not start with a clearly defined aim. It emerges as the journey proceeds. Sometimes we sense that we have taken a wrong turn by experiencing ourselves as less functional, less alive, less perspicuous. Avoiding these turns helps to guide us in settling upon interim aims along the way.

T: So there seems to be no particular standards by which we can judge the life-process.

S: There are no particular standards that extend over a whole journey or ones that necessarily hold between journeys. But particular standards arise from within a journey, which may include valuing life-processes as such. In any case, we cannot choose between journeys from a "disinterested" point of view, since we are always already in some journey.

T: But if we are ever to get anywhere, we must know what we are aiming for, even if that changes. The suggestion that the aim is in the process does not help when you are faced with the actual problem of creating something. Your view is not going to help us much when you want to know what to do next.

S: The process-centered view is not meant to provide particular aims within the journey. And, for that matter, your product-centered view does not do so either. While we do need interim aims in the journey, the journey as such needn't be going toward any specific place in particular. Nor need we project a particular place to motivate the journeying.

While product-centered and process-centered personal programs may be ramified in different ways, several general observations can be made about them. First, there appears no conclusive way of adjudicating between them, since, at the least, the very question of whether there are common standards in virtue of which such adjudication can be made out is itself a point of contention between them. Reasons offered in justification of a personal program are internal to the standards implicated by the program in question. Each operates according to different standards, and they are incongruent. There appears to be no single ideally admissible personal program. Of course, one may adduce good reasons for holding one or the other program, but doing so does not unseat the other as unreasonable, inappropriate, or inapt. Clearly, inconclusiveness does not render the choice of personal program either arbitrary or irrational. Second, the pursuit of either of these personal programs will foster different kinds of lives. Third, these personal programs compete with each other on the condition that they assume a sufficiently common object-of-interpretation, namely an ideal way of life. But, were such commonality to be denied, there would be no competition between them. And one can well imagine pluralizing the object-of-interpretation by suggesting that, while the process-centered view addresses itself to one sort of life, the product-centered view addresses itself to a quite different sort of life; and such sorts of life are not common. Again, the matter is contestable.

Certain personal programs appear to be more appropriately adopted within particular cultural settings, and this point will bear on our discussion of imputational interpretation of other cultures. For example, the product-centered program is more appropriately embraced in a highly acquisitive product-centered culture, like that of the contemporary United States. Embracing a process-centered personal program in such a culture may give rise to a kind of psychological or social dissonance. Yet clearly one's personal program is not strictly necessitated by prevailing cultural values. In turn, the process-centered personal program appears to be more appropriately adopted in a process-centered culture like that of the Hopi Indians, whose very language reflects a process-oriented view of things. Or it might be more appropriately adopted by such peoples as the Tibetan Buddhists who understand products to be merely nominal existents and impermanent. Correspondingly they disvalue the mere production of things. As well, insofar as they are *personal* programs, such programs function more pointedly in cultures of pronounced individuality, where, as in guilt cultures, the personal or the individual is emphasized. This is the case in characteristic Western cultures. But it is not the case in those cultures where the personal or the individual is less pronounced, as in such shame cultures as tribal Africa or certain Asian communities. Any personal program, as a *personal* program, would function in a less pointed way, if at all, in such settings

The imputational interpretations of individual selves one finds in psychotherapy are related to personal programs. As Roy Schafer suggests, in a therapeutic context the analysand and the analyst jointly construct a narrative based upon descriptions of episodes accepted as salient in the analysand's ongoing narrative.[27] Formulating such a narrative satisfies the dual purpose of making sense of the analysand's history and of helping to guide future choices. The analysand makes his or her memories intelligible by casting them in terms of the pertinent narrative. At the same time, "the same" memories could be cast in different terms, depending upon their place in different narratives. And there is no neutral overarching standard in virtue of which to conclusively adjudicate among narratives. As in the case of the artist reconstructing the history of his or her artistic corpus with the aid of a personal program, a reconstructed psychonarrative can guide subsequent phases in the analysand's emerging life. Correspondingly, Donald Spence affirms that generally the notion of a past actuality—as it actually was—can play no praxial role in the determination of acceptable psychoanalytic interpretations.[28] Rather, that question can be addressed only inconclusively by evaluating the narratives in which the interpretations appear.

In speaking of imputation I have considered personal programs as kinds of interpretations of life-processes, and life-processes as objects-of-interpretation. I have also been speaking of individual selves as objects-of-interpretation. Yet one might suggest that life-processes or individual selves are not objects-of-interpretation on a par with, say, musical works or works of art. Quite so. There are significant dif-

27. See Roy Schafer, "Action and Narration in Psychoanalysis," *New Literary History* (1980), 61–85; see also his "Narration in the Psychoanalytic Dialogue," *Critical Inquiry* (Autumn 1980), 29–53.
28. Donald P. Spence, *Narrative Truth and Historical Truth: Meaning and Interpretation in Psychoanalysis* (New York: Norton, 1984).

ferences between them. But such differences do not prohibit them from being circumscribed as objects-of-interpretation. Just as there is no a priori constraint on what sort of thing may be circumscribed as a work of art (consider conceptual art or process art) there is no a priori constraint on what sort of thing may be circumscribed as an object-of-interpretation. But even if one were to disallow the phrase "object-of-interpretation" for life-processes or for individual selves, or even if one were to disallow that they might be interpreted, programs pertaining to life-processes and psychonarratives exemplify imputation. As well, there is no overarching standard in virtue of which one personal program or psychonarrative may be shown to be conclusively right. In any case, whether or not inconclusivity is here exemplified in interpretation, it is not only in interpretation that such inconclusivity may obtain.

Let us now consider imputational interpretation in the interpretation of other cultures. Charles Taylor says: "We have to admit that inter-subjective social reality has to be partly defined in terms of meanings; that meanings as subjective are not just in causal interaction with a social reality made up of brute data, but that as inter-subjective they are constitutive of this reality."[29]

So, on Taylor's view, social reality is constituted or imputed by intersubjective meaning, and there is no personal or social order autonomous of intersubjective constitution. There is no metaphysically subsisting social reality prior to or autonomous of that which is intersubjectively constituted. It should be clear that Taylor is not speaking of personal or social identity in a spatiotemporal sense.

At the same time, the ways in which social reality is constituted may well be incongruent or incommensurable. Taylor says:

> With changes in his self-definition go changes in what man is, such that he has to be understood in different terms. But the conceptual mutations in human history can and frequently do produce conceptual webs which are incommensurable, that is, where the terms cannot be defined in relation to a common stratum of expressions. The entirely different notions of bargaining in our society and in some primitive ones provide an example. Each will be glossed in

29. Taylor, *Philosophy and the Human Sciences*, p. 38.

terms of practices, institutions, and ideas in each society which have nothing corresponding to them in the other.[30]

While different cultures may be incommensurable in the ways Taylor describes, they are not incomparable. No alternative culture can be so different from that of an interpreter's home culture that it is completely unintelligible. That is, while there may be no common standards for conclusive ranking, critical comparison between cultures remains possible. Understandability is not coextensive with translatability.

For example, we can understand the reasonableness of polygamy in tribal Kenya to the extent that we can make sense of marital arrangements generally, and to the extent to which we can make sense of the need for many children as a work force in an agrarian setting. Further, we can make sense of the idea that in such a setting the number of children one has serves as a sign of power and prestige. That practice also arises from the view that men's sexual enjoyment, procreation, and emotional intimacy are distinct and may be expressed with different female partners. On the other hand, Western Christians hold that polygamy is not a rationally adoptable marital arrangement, given their view of fidelity that closely associates procreation, emotional intimacy, and sexual enjoyment—all motivated by a distinctive view about the relation of persons to a Christian God. The justification of each of these views is provided in terms local and internal to the forms of life there embodied. The respective understandings of polygamy by the Western interpreter and the African interpreter are shaped by the fact that each understands it in terms of concepts that are intelligible in his or her home culture.

The shareability of such concepts is not unproblematic, however. Consider the case of incest. On a first gloss, one might see no barrier to a European interpreter making sense of tribal Kenyan prohibitions against incest. Indeed, it appears to be a cultural invariant. Yet it is unclear that what is emically (that is, intentionally) meant by incest is the same in all cultures. While the injunction—in one form or another, that a father should not have sexual relations with his daugh-

---

30. Ibid., p. 55.

ter—might be a cultural universal, what is understood as the meaning of incestuous behavior differs between cultures. Put otherwise, as the following example will show, abstinence may be abstinence from something that is glossed in one way in one culture while glossed in a distinctly different way in another culture. Although there may be no a priori barrier to one's coming to understand the meaning of incest in alternative cultures, one should be careful not to assume that sameness of "etic" external behavior constitutes sameness of "emic" intentional meaning.

More specifically, for the East African Luo tribesman the sin of incest is understood in tandem with the sin of homosexuality and with the sin of interfering with another's fate.[31] All three sins fall under the collecting concept of "Kira," for which there is no analogue in Judeo-Christian moral discourse. This covering concept of Kira collects all worst sins in the Luo morality. To be sure, a Western interpreter can come to understand this discourse (as here evidenced). But when, for example Luo medicineman Tago Athieno characterizes the sins of Kira as "unthinkable," he poses something of a puzzle for the Western interpreter who can, for example, readily think incest, homosexuality, or interfering with another fate, all as "thinly described."[32] What he perhaps cannot think are these "sins" as "thickly described" in a Luo context, that is, thoughts in which such acts are not thinkable. The western interpreter may not think such acts insofar as doing so would involve thinking how the fiber of Luo communal life would thereby be rent. Luo morality is in the first instance communal morality, and the sins of Kira are sins for their communal damage. This communalism is characteristic of shame cultures generally. And perhaps Tago Athieno cannot think of homosexual relations, for example, in the individualistic terms so characteristically implicated in Western guilt cultures. Generally, as Margaret Mead suggested, a guilt cultural interpretation will construe social behavior in such terms as to assign moral responsibility to individuals whose

---

31. See the Appendix, which is a transcript of a portion of an interview of Tago Athieno, Kenyan Luo medicineman, in which the Luo view of incest is discussed.

32. I am here using Clifford Geertz's well-known distinction between thick and thin descriptions. See his "Thick Description: Toward an Interpretive Theory of Culture," in *The Interpretation of Cultures* (New York: Basic Books, 1973).

consciences (or some cognate thereof) are implicated in some way. On the other hand, a shame cultural interpretation will construe social behavior in such terms as to assign moral responsibility to the collective, regarding the individual as an extension of the collective.

There appears to be no overarching and non–question-begging standard in virtue of which guilt cultural interpretations and shame cultural interpretations might be adjudicated. Standards appropriate for one interpretation are not fully translatable into standards appropriate for the other. Yet, as I suggested in Chapter 2 and will further develop in Chapter 4, incommensurability does not rule out understandability or rational comparability. While there may be contingent psychological or anthropological barriers to understanding alternative cultures there are no barriers of principle which would rule out, say, a Western interpreter immersing him or herself in a shame cultural context, so that he or she could come to see how homosexual acts, for example, could be unthinkable for the Luo. And the point may be made the other way around as well. There appears no barrier in principle to an interpreter from a shame culture immersing him or herself in a guilt cultural context to see the matter otherwise. Again, non-translatability does not preclude understandability.

But the matter may be yet more complex. It might be that Tago Athieno would have no principled difficulty in coming to understand the sins of Kira in the terms that a Westerner might. But successfully conducting such an experiment—that is, seeing the situation from a guilt cultural perspective—might require him to project himself in a cultural context so different from his own that it would be an open question whether he could, in that scenario, continue to recognize himself as the culturally embodied person he is. And the converse might also hold true for a European interpreter. In this way an interpreter may well be constrained by his self-conception in just such acts of thought or imagination. While Tago Athieno and I may come to understand each other, it remains an open question whether when we do so we continue to have the same sense of ourselves as the culturally embodied selves that we were. In the extreme, one might even be tempted to question whether it was the initial "we" who had come to understand and be understood after all. Consequently, for me to occupy Tago Athieno's interpretive place or for him to occupy mine may not, as a matter of fact, be live options for us.

Such complexities aside, what a shame cultural interpreter and what a guilt cultural interpreter might talk about may differ, but perhaps not sufficiently so to prohibit them from agreeing that they have different interpretations of a sufficiently common or "unicitous" object-of-interpretation: incest. Yet such an agreement would not be based on an appeal to some neutral, acultural point of view, or to some idea of a realistic practice-independent phenomenon—one independent of any specific cultural context. Although cultural comparisons are inevitably formulated within the terms of the interpreter's home culture, this situation does not preclude the possibility of enriching such terms so as to learn from the confrontation of cultures, itself understood from an ever reconstituted and expanded vantage point.

Now, if self-understanding or other-understanding involves self-interpretation or other-interpretation, and if self-interpretation or other-intrepretation involves imputing or constituting ourselves or others, then—as the objects-of-interpretation in question—the resultant selves or others are candidates for pluralizing or aggregating. Put otherwise, it is an open question whether the emerging selves or others are common or unicitous. In such matters there appears to be no fact of the matter about who "we" really are. In such matters, as Clifford Geertz says, "Societies, like lives, contain their own interpretations."[33]

In this chapter I have sketched how imputational interpretation might be exemplified in diverse cases. Clearly each one could well be the subject of an extended study in its own right. But the broad outlines of the imputationalist view have emerged: in imputational

---

33. Ibid., p. 453. The matter is made yet more interesting when we consider the Buddhist suggestion that the very distinction between self and other is imputed, and, according to that program, it is one which should be overcome for enlightenment. See, for example, (Lama) Anagarika Govinda, *The Psychological Attitude of Early Buddhist Philosophy* (Delhi: Motilal Banarsidass, 1991), esp. part IV. On existence, imputation, and the Buddhist rejection of "inherent existence," see (His Holiness the Dalai Lama) Tenzin Gyatso, *Cultivating a Daily Meditation* (Dharmsala, India: Library of Tibetan Works and Archives, 1991).

interpretation what is taken as the object-of-interpretation is a function of the interpretation under consideration. And, whether we accept one interpretation over another is not so much a matter of the fit between an interpretation and an autonomous or practice-independent object-of-interpretation, but rather a matter of the fit between an interpretation and the object-of-interpretation construed in the light of the interpretation in question. So, to accept one interpretation over another is to accept one interpretive package over another.

Keeping these examples in mind, let us now elaborate the imputationalist view and consider it in light of anti-imputationalist criticisms.

4

Imputation and the Comparison of Interpretations

Before developing the idea of imputational interpretation in the face of anti-imputationalist criticisms we should reiterate that although the acceptance of the thesis of imputational interpretation would add substantial support for multiplism, multiplism does not require imputational interpretation. Multiplism obtains, at least, on the condition that for competing interpretations there are no overarching standards for their conclusive ranking. Imputational interpretation provides a special case for that condition. If imputational interpretation were to be found unacceptable, though, that would not by itself unseat the multiplist claim. Now, keeping in mind our discussion in Chapter 3 of imputational interpretation in art, poetry, persons, and cultures, let us proceed to consider imputational interpretation more fully.

Imputationalism and Its Criticisms

The imputationalist view holds that cultural entities are the class of their interpretations, and that there is no object-of-interpretation independent of interpretation as such. The object-of-interpretation has no structure independent of interpretation as such. What is interpreted is not constituted independently of interpretation; interpretation constitutes objects-of-interpretations. While the imputationalist view holds that an object-of-interpretation is not independent of interpretation as such, this does not necessarily mean that any particular interpretation on a given occasion may fully constitute its object-of interpretation. That would be a radical kind of imputationalism and would indeed invite arbitrariness. The radical version should be contrasted with a more moderate imputationalism (to be considered in the remainder of this book) according to which a given object-of-interpretation may be constituted within webs of interpretations with more or less complex histories. Imputational interpretation involves selecting features of the presented materials with which to fashion an object-of-interpretation. Imputational interpretation is not spun of nothing nor are there no constraints on it. It is constrained by the materials provided within the context of a pertinent practice. The imputationalist view holds that cultural entities are capable of being transformed through history. It allows for the imputation of properties to objects-of-interpretation over interpretive moments. Everything we interpret has a history, and is altered by the history of its interpretations.

Now, since there may be an infinite number of interpretive moments, there may also be an infinite number of interpretations. But according to the imputationalist view, this possibility does not entail that there are no constraints on the range of ideally admissible interpretations at any particular historical moment. There may be a handful of ideally admissible interpretations at any given moment.

In contrast, the anti-imputationalist view of interpretation holds that objects-of-interpretation are fully constituted independently of interpretation as such. Objects-of-interpretation are quite distinct from interpretation. They cannot be constituted by interpretation. Whichever interpretations are admissible must be constrained by something other than interpretation itself. Opposing the imputationalist, the anti-imputationalist view holds that if an interpretation fully constitutes its objects-of-interpretation, there would be a population explosion of objects-of-interpretation. Consequently, no two interpretations of a given object-of-interpretation could compete. Objects-of-interpretation would multiply by the number of interpretations offered. Further, the anti-imputationalist holds that it must be possible for an interpretation to be wrong or inadmissible, and this possibility implies that interpretations cannot impute their own objects-of-interpretation. The anti-imputationalist holds that it must be possible to identify and reidentify objects-of-interpretation on different occasions, and charges that the imputationalist is unable to satisfy this requirement. And, for interpretations to explain objects-of-interpretation and not be just responsive to them, objects-of-interpretation must be autonomous.

The anti-imputationalist holds further that one should not, at a given time or over a period of time, allow infinitely many interpretations of cultural entities—be those interpretations formalist, psychoanalytic, feminist, or whatever. The object-of-interpretation should not be merely an occasion to project interpretations, but should be explained by an interpretation. The admissible interpretation should capture the work's real nature, independent of interpretation.

The anti-imputationalist may concede that every act of interpretation is situated in a historical and cultural background; and that interpretations of texts of various kinds have changed throughout history. But he or she may insist that making this acknowledgment does not require embracing the general conclusion that an interpretation is historically bounded. The anti-imputationalist is concerned that, on the imputationalist account, the object-of-interpretation is reduced to the status of a Rorschach inkblot, into which interpreters may read anything that might otherwise occupy them.

The anti-imputationalist urges that without some account of objects-of-interpretation independent of interpretation, one could not say whether an interpretation was faithful to the object-of-interpretation. The idea of fidelity would drop out, and with it so would the touchstone for admissibility.

The differences between the imputationalist and the anti-imputationalist views may be brought out by considering the fact that post-dictively one characteristically comes to see the plausibility of certain views with the advantage of new vocabularies and theories developed in intervening periods. In this way, a certain interpretation might come to be seen as more or less reasonable than previously. For example, this would be true of pre- and post-Marxist writings, or pre- and post-Freudian writings, or, indeed, writings before and after any significant cultural intervention. The anti-imputationalist might well concede that people may indeed come to see the same things differently under different historical circumstances. But he or she holds that that fact has nothing to do with constituting or reconstituting an object-of-interpretation. Rather, such facts bear on the history of culture in that they document the different ways in which different people come to see the same things. Objects-of-interpretation should have real stability, which is in no way parasitic upon interpretation as such.

We should note that the anti-imputationalist and the imputationalist agree that one should be historically responsible in settling upon ideally admissible interpretations. But the very construal of historical considerations is itself contentious in just the the ways already indicated. The appeal to historical authenticity does not advance the discussion, for the imputationalist versus anti-imputationalist controversy reenters the discussion about historical interpretation itself. (See Chapter 6).

While the anti-imputationalist might charge that the thesis of infinite interpretations amounts to anarchism, that thesis is in fact consistent with the claim that, at any given time, there may be constraints on what interpretations are ideally admissible or on what is admissibly imputable. It is only from a more global point of view that the claim of infinite interpretations is made out to start with. From a local point of view, the range of ideally admissible interpretations is not infinite. Structurally, the situation looks rather like this: Any given set has a limited number of points in it. And there are an infinite number of sets. It follows, therefore, that globally there are an infinite number of points. But, in the context of actually settling upon admissible interpretations in a given historical moment, the range is not infinitely open. So, in the end, the imputationalist and the anti-imputationalist may well agree that some interpretations of a given object-of-interpretation at a certain historical moment are inadmissible. Again, rejecting the view that there is one single right interpretation of a work does not entail anarchism. There are intermediary stages which may constrain what is admissible at a particular time.

There is nothing in the imputationalist's program—again, of the more moderate kind—that bars constraints on those who impute or construct. It is hospitable to a range of constraints such as those barring logical contradiction, incoherence, and—as we saw in the case of music—irrational reconstructions of the traditions out of which pertinent objects-of-interpretation and their interpretations arose. The imputationalist's view of interpretation does not mandate that just anyone on any occasion may do just any constituting or imputing. So, the inference from imputationalism to anarchism is invalid. Indeed, to avoid anarchism one should not allow that a given object-of-interpretation may answer to both a globally infinite and a *locally unrestricted* number of possible interpretations. One should not allow the imputing or constituting of separate objects-of-interpretation for each interpretation. Otherwise, we would find ourselves in something like a world of Babel, where we could not agree or disagree about anything at all, but just talk past one another. Yet, again, there is nothing in the imputationalist's program that bars the possibility of gradual rather than radical imputation, one that is historically evolutionary rather than single-person or single-occasion revolutionary. Indeed, the possibility of gradual rather than radical imputation of cultural entities allows that they may be products of interpretation per se, yet not that they may be fully imputed at a particular moment.

Notice that according to radical imputationalism, commonality or unicity between objects-of-interpretation with would-be competing interpretations is ruled out, since according to this view an interpretation always constructs its own unique object-of-interpretation. Such construction would be tantamount to radically pluralizing objects-of-interpretation. Consequently radical imputationalism would be incompatible with multiplism. It might appear that radical imputationalism entails singularism. For any apparently competing pair of interpretations, the conflict would be dissipated by way of the pluralizing maneuver. But in such circumstances the single admissible interpretation that would have resulted could not have survived *after* ranking some potential candidates. No alternative candidates could have been considered from the start. Thus, singularism of a critical sort—that is, one in which critical comparison would be possible at all—would have been disallowed by radical imputationalism. In this way, radical imputationalism entails an impoverished kind of singularism, for, as anticipated in Chapter 1, praxial ideality generally, and singularism specifically, are understood in the context of the possibility of competition between interpretations.

One might remark that the thesis of imputational interpretation involves one in an objectionable circularity between imputing interpretations and their objects-of-interpretation. Yet, as we have seen, the circularity is benign. Imputational interpretation does not license the imputation of an entire unique object-of-interpretation on any given occasion. It does not license the imputation of just anything on any occasion. For example, in the musical case, the score is understood within a historical context. It is embedded in a practice that is historically entrenched. Imputational interpretation does not entail the view that one can fully make or remake a score on any given occasion. The score is accepted as a constraint—more or less invariantly between contending interpretations—on the range of ideally admissible interpretations. To allow that interpretations should impute properties to their objects-of-interpretation is not to allow that there are no constraints on what is admissibly imputable.

In passing, we should note that the distinction between an interpretation and its object-of-interpretation cannot always be practically drawn. Artists, for example, both symbiotically create and interpret their own works in progress. Indeed, such symbiosis may be so organically connected that creation and interpretation might not be distinguishable. What might appear to be a clear division of labor between the artist on the one hand and the art historian or critic on the other hand has no straightforward analogue for the artist who is both creator and interpreter. The division of labor between artist and art historian or critic may falsely represent an irreducibly complex phenomenon for the creative artist.

David Novitz, for one, resists any imputational function to interpretation. He characterizes "two quite distinct" senses of interpretation and rejects as fanciful one sense which would be imputational. He distinguishes:

> one in which interpretations involve conjectures intended to answer certain questions or solve certain puzzles, and another in which interpretations involve the fanciful, largely subjective, and entirely

gratuitous elaboration of the work. The trouble is that in speaking of interpretation we sometimes confuse these two senses. For performances of concert pianists, for instance, are frequently regarded as interpretations—where this may mean two quite different things. In some cases pianists perform, and so interpret, certain works without attempting to solve any specific puzzles or answer any questions about the work. Theirs is an elaborative contribution to the work: they merely weave their fanciful variations within the "limits" of the score, and so come to perform the work in ways which they regard as straightforward and uncontrived. There are, however, situations in which pianists may quite properly be puzzled about how best to play a piece, and in these cases their performances (interpretations) involve problem-solving of one sort or another. Confusion between these two kinds of interpretations is encouraged by the fact that they often (quite contingently) affect each other. Interpretive problem-solving may be strongly influenced by one's (interpretive) elaboration of a work, while one's elaborations, in their turn, may be influenced by one's answers to earlier questions or puzzles. But all of this is a reason for emphasizing, not blurring the distinction between these two types of interpretation.[1]

Yet imputational interpretation may or may not be solving a puzzle. An interpretation may impute properties to its object-of-interpretation without at the same time being "an entirely gratuitous elaboration of the work." The distinction between anti-imputational and imputational interpretation is not coextensive with Novitz's distinction between puzzle-solving and fanciful gratuitous interpretation.

But Novitz goes on to charge that imputational interpretation commits objects-of-interpretation to a state of unacceptable instability. By way of attack he rehearses Margolis's view, saying:

> On Margolis's view...works of art are incomplete, and the task of completing them falls to those who attend to, and wish to understand, the works. The resultant interpretations are said to involve "a touch of virtuosity, an element of performance," for in interpreting a literary work of art the reader is required to imagine properties which can plausibly be imputed to the work, and which

---

1. David Novitz, *Knowledge, Fiction, and Imagination* (Philadelphia: Temple University Press, 1987), pp. 91–92.

in being imputed, actually become a part of it.... Margolis is of the opinion that these interpretations are importantly, indeed vitally, influenced by that cultural baggage that each individual brings to the work, and since not everyone carries the same baggage, the view is that at least some of the properties of an artwork are inherently unstable.[2]

Novitz's restatement of the imputationalist view is substantially correct, and here we may note that Novitz rightly understands that, according to the view, in imputing properties to a work, such properties "actually become a part of it." Put otherwise, such properties become intrinsic to the object-of-interpretation. And interpretations are influenced by the cultural baggage that interpreters bring to the work. But, again, such influence should not be taken as amounting to subjectivism or anarchism. An interpreter is not free to choose his cultural baggage *tout court*. If Margolis defends the intentionality of cultural objects-of-interpretation, he emphasizes social and not individual intentionality. Of course, because the conditions of imputation vary, that which is imputed is unstable. But such instability is benign.

Ironically, Novitz's counter-suggestion actually concedes as much.

> On my view, all objects, and not just "culturally freighted" ones, are perceived in terms of cultural "myths" of one sort or another—although this, it should be emphasized, does not commit me to any relativism whatsoever. Margolis's mistake is to suppose that these "myths" are chronically unstable, for they plainly are not. They are often enduring and form part of those stabilities which help characterize a society and its culture. It is our knowledge of these stabilities which allows us to discern and describe the properties of the (natural and cultural) objects which surround us.[3]

Here Novitz unwittingly concedes Margolis's point. He allows that whatever stabilities obtain are a function of "cultural myths" currently in place. In turn, the stabilities are historically contingent. It appears then that the difference between these authors is not philosophical at all, but a difference concerning whether pertinent cultural myths

2. Ibid., p. 114.
3. Ibid., p. 115.

"slide" all that much over historical time. They actually agree that the stability of an object-of-interpretation depends upon its praxial context, and that it is historically variable.

Now, one might think that the imputationalist view opposes my attitude of agnosticism with respect to ontological issues. But it should be recalled that in formulating my agnostic attitude with respect to ontological issues I have in mind a fairly restricted notion of the ontological, namely, that concerning ontological realism or ontological constructionism. So, when advancing the view that one may impute or constitute objects-of-interpretation, one may well remain agnostic about whether or not there is some identifiable object independent of interpretive practice.

In this regard the anti-imputationalist's resistance to the imputationalist program may be motivated by a mistakenly inflated view about the robustness of what the imputationalist takes to be imputed. The imputationalist is making a claim about nominal existents, and leaves aside the question of any putative relation between such existents and other possibly more robust existents. The imputationalist is concerned to affirm the imputation of nominal existents. And this claim is different from the one that ontologically real existents can be brought about by imputation. The imputationalist makes no such grandiose claim. Nor is he or she tempted to do so, for the imputationalist resists the ontological realist program to start with.

Thus far in this chapter I have considered the view that interpretation may have an imputational function in characteristic cultural practices. But the overriding argument for multiplism—namely, that there is a multiplicity of interpretation practices without overarching standards for their adjudication—does not depend upon the imputational view. That overriding argument faces the question of the grounds for critical comparison between contending interpretations. It is to that question that I now turn. I shall return to questions of the identity and determinacy of objects-of-interpretation in Part II.

Inconclusivity and Good Reasons

I have characterized singularism and multiplism in terms of conclusivity and inconclusivity, which concern the presence or absence of overarching adjudicating standards. As I have said, these logical conditions should be contrasted with decisiveness and indecisiveness, which are psychological conditions. The latter distinction bears on the strength of one's resolve to embrace a particular view. Of course, one may be decisive about what is conclusive; and one may be indecisive about what is inconclusive. But decisiveness need not be matched by conclusivity. One may be indecisive in one's resolve to embrace what is conclusively mandated; and one may be decisive in one's resolve to embrace what is inconclusively mandated. Conclusivity or inconclusivity may obtain with respect to ranking interpretations or with respect to ranking standards for ranking interpretations. So, while two competing interpretations may be conclusively ranked in the presence of an adjudicating standard, it need not follow that the operative standard is itself conclusively mandated by a yet further overarching standard.

A singularist might wish to stop what he or she thinks could be a pernicious infinite regress of levels of standards by stipulating that some standards arise from first principles—that they are self-evident, or that they embody an absolute order of reality or real essences or real human nature, or something of the sort. Such first principles would generate the pertinent standards and would require no further justification. For such first principles, the question of justification (that might invoke yet further standards) cannot arise.

Now, while some starting stipulations and assumptions are always pragmatically necessary to get on with a given inquiry or practice there is no reason in principle why they may not themselves become the objects of further consideration. That there might be ever yet further competing stipulations and assumptions cannot be ruled out in principle. Correspondingly, the possibility of inconclusivity is forever open, even though for pragmatic purposes we must close this possibility depending upon particular needs and interests. As R. G. Collingwood urged, that which is taken as an "absolute presupposition" is itself historically variable.[4]

Inconclusiveness obtains where, in the absence of a standard to rank interpretations A and B, interpretation A cannot be said to be

---

4. R. G. Collingwood, *An Essay on Metaphysics* (Oxford: Clarendon Press, 1949).

better than, worse than, or equal to interpretation B. Inconclusiveness further obtains where the present standards are not collectable under an overarching standard in virtue of which they may be ranked. If we think of Muti's interpretation as one of a kind whose standard is aesthetic consistency, for example, we may judge whether his is better than, worse than, or equal to another interpretation whose standard is also aesthetic consistency. Alternatively, if we think of Comissiona's interpretation as one of a kind whose standard is absolute faithfulness to the score, we may judge whether his is better than, worse than, or equal to another interpretation whose standard is also such faithfulness. Saying this much need not lead us to hold that, according to an overarching standard, those interpretations which embrace aesthetic consistency are better than, worse than, or equal to those kinds of interpretation which embrace absolute faithfulness to the score. Yet, within this space one can provide critical comparison and good reasons for one's preferences.

More formally, in this case we cannot conclude that A1 is better than, worse than, or equal to B1, for the reason that it is open as to whether A-kinds are better than, worse than, or equal to B-kinds. So long as A-kinds and B-kinds are not rankable by a common standard, they are incommensurable. But, clearly, if A-kinds and B-kinds are not rankable it does not follow that no interesting comparative remarks can be made about A1 and B1. Of course, were one to say some such thing as that an A-kind is *inherently* better than a B-kind (say, that aesthetic consistency is inherently better than faithfulness to the score), then one would effect a commensurability. But such a claim would be most implausible for the kinds of cases considered here.

More fully, good reasons may be offered for preferring a given interpretation based on local standards (Muti's interpretation, say, with respect to aesthetic consistency). And if an alternative interpretation is justified by an alternative local standard (Comissiona's interpretation, say, with respect to faithfulness to the score), that does not unseat the first interpretation as inadmissible. The preference for each interpretation may be justified for local reasons, that is, reasons in accord with local standards in the absence of overarching standards. Further, multiplism allows that one may for good reasons prefer one interpretation over another (Muti's, say, over André Previn's with respect to aesthetic consistency; or Comissiona's over Muti's with respect to faithfulness to the score). In this respect the multiplist does not concede to the singularist that the less preferred interpretation according to a given standard should not be ideally admissible. Good reasons would be relativized to the standards pertinent to the respective interpretation. Yet critical comparison and good reasons for preferences (say, between Muti's and Comissiona's interpretations) do not require ranking according to a common standard.

One might object that if a reason does not determine whether A is better than, worse than, or equal to B it is not a reason. But this need not be so, for a good reason may provide understanding for one's preference for A or B or neither. Providing the rationale for one's preferences is not the same thing as providing grounds for the judgment that A is better than, worse than, or equal to B. In this sense a good reason may answer the question whether it is it reasonable to prefer A, B, or neither, rather than whether A is better than, worse than, or equal to B.

A similar account can be given of interpretation in other cultural practices. While a Marxist interpretation of Van Gogh's *Potato Eaters* may be better than a psychological interpretation with respect to its power to reveal the relations of economic institutions embodied in it, a psychological interpretation may be better than a Marxist interpretation with respect to its power to reveal the character of its leading figures. With respect to each of these standards one can reasonably say that one interpretation is better than the other, or vice versa. But, since there is no overarching standard to rank these standards, one can give reasons only for preferring a particular Marxist interpretation over a particular psychological interpretation.

Now one might object that, local or not, justificationism as such (in this case, of preferences) is unacceptable. For example, a follower of Karl Popper's negativist epistemology might hold that justification is a kind of induction. And induction is logically impotent. Thus, the Popperian might hold that there are no justifying good reasons *for* anything, only good reasons *against* things. But by disallowing justification—that is, providing good reasons—the Popperian undercuts his own position. The very argument that falsification is logically stronger than verification (the method of induction) itself constitutes a good reason for the view that one should gear one's epistemology in a negativist way.

We should note that agreement does not guarantee commensuration, for two persons might agree, say, that A is preferable over B, while their standards differ. Agreement that A is preferable over B need not hang on any common standard. Confrontation may be averted or overcome, agreements made, and a joint course of action set without agreement on the pertinent standards. Thus, in an academic committee, or in a committee of judges who are charged with awarding a "Best of Show" prize in an art competition, agreement is no evidence that a single common standard has been deployed. Having made a decision is no guarantee that various, perhaps incongruent, standards are not in play.

Incommensurability and Comparability

One might urge that no matter what pair of incongruent standards are in place, it is always possible to introduce an overarching standard. That is, there are no genuine cases of incommensurability. The motivating thought behind such a suggestion might be that incommensurability precludes critical comparability. But it does not. So, let us consider more closely the idea of critical comparison without commensurability. First, then, let us explicate the idea of commensurability.

The *Encyclopaedia of Mathematics* defines commensurable and incommensurable magnitudes or quantities as "two magnitudes of the same kind (such as lengths or surface areas) that do or do not have a so-called common measure (that is, a magnitude of the same kind contained an integral number of times in both of them). Examples of incommensurable magnitudes are the lengths of a diagonal of a square and the sides of that square, or the surface areas of a circle and the square of its radius. If the two magnitudes are commensurable, then their ratio is a rational number, whereas the ratio of incommensurable magnitudes is irrational."[5]

Thomas Kuhn ramifies this thought in the following way:

> Remember briefly where the term 'incommensurability' came from. The hypotenuse of an isosceles right triangle is incommensurable with its side or the circumference of a circle with its radius in the sense that there is no unit of length contained without residue an integral number of times in each number of the pair. There is thus no common measure. But lack of common measure does not make comparison impossible....
>
> Applied to the conceptual vocabulary deployed in and around a scientific theory, the term 'incommensurability' functions metaphorically. The phrase 'no common measure' becomes 'no common language.' The claim that two theories are incommensurable is then the claim that there is no language, neutral or otherwise, into which both theories, conceived as sets of sentences, can be translated, without residue or loss. No more in its metaphorical than its literal form does incommensurability imply incomparability, and for much the same reason. The claim that two theories are incommensurable is more modest than many of its critics have supposed.[6]

For example, Kuhn has shown there is no full translation between the key concepts of the Aristotelian lexicon and those of contemporary physics. That discrepancy is not just a matter of not having a sufficiently worked out dictionary. Rather it results from the fact that lexical terms are semantically tied to paradigm-specific ways of looking at things. Yet we are able to compare critically Aristotelian and contemporary physics, noting how well, for example, respective sets of concepts relate to each other, how well they accommodate what each takes to be its legitimate domain, and the like. Incommensurability does not entail incomparability.

At the same time, such considerations as the ability of one set of concepts to relate to each other, or how well they accommodate what

---

5. M. Hazelwinkel, ed., *Encyclopaedia of Mathematics* (Dordrecht, 1988).
6. Thomas S. Kuhn, "Commensurability, Comparability, Communicability," *Philosophy of Science Association* 2 (1982), 670–71.

each takes to be its proper domain, may or may not be sufficiently precise to function as adjudicating standards. But if such precision is lacking, that is no reason to reject those considerations from the discussion about critical comparison or reasoned preferences among contending interpretations.

Yet the judgment whether one set of concepts is able to coherently relate to another, or whether it is able to accommodate what it takes to be its proper domain, requires a conceptual space. For example, for Kuhn to compare critically Aristotelian and contemporary physics requires a space from which he may judge pertinent considerations. What status should one attach to such a space?

Critical Comparison and the Question of Ethnocentrism

This sort of question has prompted Charles Taylor—in the context of comparing cultures—to articulate his idea of a language of perspicuous contrast. And that general instinct is right. Unfortunately, Taylor holds that such a language is culturally neutral and will help him avoid ethnocentrism. In turn, I shall suggest (with Clifford Geertz and Richard Rorty) that ethnocentrism is ineliminable.

More fully, Taylor says:

> Suppose we are trying to give an account of a society very different from our own, say a primitive society. The society has (what we call) religious and magical practices. To understand them in the strong sense would require that we come to grasp how they use the key words in which they praise and blame, describe what they yearn for or seek, what they abhor and fear, and so on. Understanding their religious practices would require that we come to understand what they see themselves as doing when they are carrying out the ritual we have provisionally identified as a 'sacrifice,' what they seek after in the state we may provisionally identify as 'blessedness' or 'union with the spirits'. (Our provisional identifications, of course, just place their actions/states in relation to our religious tradition, or ones familiar to us. If we stick with these, we may fall into the most distorted ethnocentric readings.) We have no way of

knowing that we have managed to penetrate their world in this way short of finding that we are able to use their key words in the same way they do, and that means that we grasp their desirability characterizations.[7]

Correspondingly, Taylor introduces his idea of a language of perspicuous contrast:

> It will *almost always* be the case that the adequate language in which we can understand another society is not our language of understanding, or theirs, but rather what one could call a language of perspicuous contrast. This would be a language in which we could formulate both their way of life and ours as alternative possibilities in relation to *some human constants* at work in both. It would be a language in which the possible human variations would be so formulated that our form of life and theirs could be perspicuously described as alternative such variations. Such a language of contrast might show their language of understanding to be distorted or inadequate in some respects, or it might show ours to be so (in which case, we might find that understanding them leads to an alteration of our self-understanding, and hence our form of life—a far from unknown process in history); or it might show both to be so.[8]

Notice, first, that Taylor's claim ("it will almost always be the case") is not a universal one. Second, Taylor ties his idea of a language of perspicuous contrast to some human constants, but it is unclear what status such constants should have. One wonders, for example, whether such human constants are themselves grounded in an ahistorical ontology or if they are historically contingent. To affirm that they are describable in a culturally neutral language—as Taylor's view suggests—would beg the question. Further, noting appropriate contrasts does not require an overarching standard or a culturally neutral language, one separate from the interpreter's original language. Rather, it involves a ramification or extension of the first language. In other words, making critical comparison, as is so characteristically

---

7. Charles Taylor, *Philosophy and the Human Sciences: Philosophical Papers*, vol. 2 (Cambridge: Cambridge University Press, 1985), pp. 120–21.
8. Ibid., p. 125–26. The emphases are mine.

done in ethnographic studies, does not require appeal to or fabrication of yet another putatively neutral language. The language of perspicuous contrast amounts to no third distinct language besides those of the interpreters and the subjects. It is really an enrichment or ramification of the interpreter's original language. Put still otherwise, to say that the interpreter's horizon has been expanded is not to say that it is the interpreter's no longer. So seen, Taylor's remark that "it will frequently be the case that we cannot understand another society until we have understood ourselves better as well," turns out to be an invitation to expand the horizons of our own language, not one to engage in an alternative language.[9] Thus, contrary to Taylor's stated intentions, ethnocentrism is affirmed rather than eliminated. Taylor's posited language of perspicuous contrast turns out not to be neutral. Nor is it something other than the interpreter's own language. Thus, the idea of a language of perspicuous contrast does not sidestep ethnocentrism.

While Taylor seeks to compare cultures in his posited language of perspicuous contrast, another strategy for commensuration suggests itself. It capitalizes on the overlap between home and alternative languages without assuming human constants. Jitendra Mohanty, for example, suggests that ever greater areas of translatability between languages can be developed based upon initially more limited areas of overlap.[10] This is a more promising suggestion, if we keep in mind that what is thought to be an alternative language is ineliminably conceived as such from within one's home language. All that such attempts can yield is the expansion of one's home language. Try as one might, no "transcendental" space can be occupied. But this overlap model may be too strong if it promises commensurating standards. For critical comparison it is enough to establish grounds common enough for communication between conversational partners, and these grounds might include shared values or norms but not adjudicating standards. In turn, a conversational model does not assume that commonality or overlap of languages pre-exists, waiting to be

---

9. Ibid., p. 129.
10. Jitendra Mohanty, "Phenomenological Rationality and the Overcoming of Relativism," in Michael Krausz, ed., *Relativism: Interpretation and Confrontation* (Notre Dame: Notre Dame University Press, 1989).

discovered.[11] Here the commonalities of languages are constituted by partners who improvise as their conversation unfolds. This approach avoids the artificial claim of neutrality, and it accommodates the Davidsonian thought that we cannot know about an alternative language more than what can be made sense of from within a home language. And it accommodates the thought that whatever universals there are are intelligibly projectable from within the bounds of one's home language.

Even the claims that there are cultural universals—for example, that all cultures exhibit linguistic competence of some sort, that all cultures exhibit self-referring indexical expressions, or that all cultures embody some moral order—are inevitably tied to the cultural conditions in which the examples are offered.[12] For example, in the cases mentioned, the very ideas of language, self-reference, and morality are tied to the cultures of the theorists who press for the corresponding universals. This is no argument against the search for universals. But it is an argument against those who think that success in identifying universals constitutes a leap to an ahistorical or transcendental understanding of cultures.

Cultural historians or cultural anthropologists, for example, who characteristically sketch the intentional contexts of past agents or culturally diverse agents must presume that their intentional terms are sufficiently similar to those of the agents being studied. The historian or anthropologist must be capable of grasping the agent's self-conception, including the agent's construal of his or her aims and methods for achieving his or her aims.[13] Yet, what the historians and anthropologists take to be intelligible already shapes the descriptions they offer of the agent's intentional situation. The historian's or the anthropologist's own intentional situation suffuses their accounts of the intentional situation of their subjects. So there can be no pre-

---

11. Bimal Krishna Matilal, "Ethical Relativism and Confrontation of Cultures," and Martha C. Nussbaum and Amartya Sen, "Internal Criticism and Indian Rationalist Traditions," both in Krausz, *Relativism*.

12. See A. Irving Hallowell, "The Self and Its Behavioural Environment," *Exploration* 2 (April 1954); Michael Carrithers, Steven Collins, and Steven Lukes, eds., *The Category of the Person* (Cambridge: Cambridge University Press, 1985); and Rom Harré, *Personal Being* (Oxford: Basil Blackwell, 1983).

13. See Collingwood, *The Idea of History* (New York: Galaxy Books, 1956).

sumption of an epistemically accessible fixed historical past actuality or an epistemically accessible fixed alternative culture. (See Chapter 6.)

Davidson puts the point this way: "speaking a language... is not a trait a man can lose while retaining the power of thought. So there is no chance that someone can take up a vantage point for comparing conceptual schemes by temporarily shedding his own."[14]

Consequences of Ethnocentrism

In the preceding section I spoke about the possibility of critical comparison between cultures within the limits of an interpreter's horizon. I suggested that ethnocentrism is ineliminable. But what are the consequences of such an ethnocentrism? Richard Rorty thinks they are radical, and he freely embraces them. He says:

> To accept the claim that there is no standpoint outside the particular historically conditioned and temporary vocabulary we are presently using from which to judge this vocabulary is to give up on the idea that there can be reasons for using languages as well as reasons within languages for believing statements. This amounts to giving up the idea that intellectual or political progress is rational, in any sense of "rational" which is neutral between vocabularies. But because it seems pointless to say that all the great moral and intellectual advances of European history—Christianity, Galilean science, the Enlightenment, Romanticism, and so on—were fortunate falls into temporary irrationality, the moral to be drawn is that the rational-irrational distinction is less useful than it once appeared. Once we realize progress, for the community as for the individual, is a matter of using new words as well as arguing from premises phrased in old words, we realize that a critical vocabulary which revolves around notions like "rational," "criteria," "argument," and "foundation" and "absolute" is badly suited to describe the relation between the old and the new.[15]

---

14. Donald Davidson, *Inquiries into Truth and Interpretation* (Oxford: Oxford University Press, 1984), p. 185.

15. Richard Rorty, *Contingency, Irony and Solidarity* (New York: Cambridge University Press, 1989), p. 48.

But this passage contains a jumble of moves which, if endorsed, brings one to face a false choice between, on the one hand, an unreconstructed philosophy that ignores the ineliminability of ethnocentrism, or, on the other hand, one that gives up any attempt at reconstructive theorizing. Rorty embraces the latter option. But from the acceptance of the claim that there is no standpoint outside the particular historically conditioned and temporary vocabulary we are presently using from which to judge this vocabulary, it simply does not follow that one must give up the idea that there can be reasons for using languages, as well as reasons formulated within those languages, for believing statements. On the contrary, such acceptance amounts to an invitation to reconstrue the very idea of good reasons which is internal to the languages in question.

So when Rorty tells us that acceding to the ethnocentrism or historicism of inquiry amounts to giving up the idea that intellectual or political progress is rational, in any sense of rational which is neutral between vocabularies, he is of course correct. But his inference from this point is quite unwarranted. He holds that since it would not do to dismiss the great advances of European history as irrational, we should abandon the rational-irrational distinction altogether. This inference begs the question by assuming that rationality should be understood in terms of neutrality. But there is no good reason to do this. Indeed, Rorty misses a promising opportunity, namely, to reconstrue the distinction between rationality and irrationality to make it compatible with ethnocentric or historicist non-neutrality. Thus, it is a non sequitur to suggest that progress (or its cognates) for the community or for the individual is vacuous. Rather, such notions as "rational," "criteria," "argument," "foundation," and "absolute" stand in need of reconstruction within an historicist framework.

In a lively encounter between Clifford Geertz and Richard Rorty, two attitudes about what both take to be the ineliminable condition of ethnocentrism are opposed.[16] That is, both agree that there is no getting away from ethnocentrism. But they handle that condition in

---

16. Clifford Geertz, "The Uses of Diversity," *Michigan Quarterly Review* (Winter 1986); and Richard Rorty, "On Ethnocentrism: A Reply to Clifford Geertz," *Michigan Quarterly Review* (Summer 1986), reprinted in Rorty, *Objectivity, Relativism, and Truth* (Cambridge: Cambridge University Press, 1991).

quite different ways. Rorty's attitude toward the ineliminability of ethnocentrism is to embrace it unapologetically and to identify himself as a white male western bourgeois liberal intellectual.[17] Liberalism of the procedural justice sort, on Rorty's view, is the best political system so far devised. Why apologize?

On the other hand, Geertz holds that ethnocentrism follows from the fact that the interpreter always interprets according to his own lights, or according to "lenses of his own grinding."[18] Who else's could they be? And, to the multiplicity of lights and lenses, he responds: the more the better. The interpreter should try to see with as many lights as possible, inevitably understood from his own at any given time. On Geertz's view, no culture with properties determinately fixed independently of interpretive practices is accessible. It is for this reason, in addition to the ineliminability of ethnocentrism, that we cannot presume to get cultural interpretations singularly right. The best that one can do, with the help of numerous lights and lenses, is to "tack in"—to use another metaphor Geertz favors—on the culture in an approximate way. At the same time, and here his attitude opposes Rorty's, Geertz takes cultural interpretation to be a vehicle for his own (and our) self-transformation or self-development. To expand one's horizon is to expand oneself. So seen, there is no *simple* way to characterize the person Clifford Geertz or any other cultural interpreter. Geertz's self-characterization as white, male, bourgeois, liberal, intellectual, and so on, resembles Rorty's self-characterization. But such a self-characterization for Geertz is *initial*, while for Rorty it is *final* in the sense that Rorty seems to see no need for self-development through confrontation with alternative cultures. Put otherwise, Geertz's ethnocentrism encourages a development in inquirers, while Rorty's does not. Cast in terms of personal programs (recall Chapter 3), we might say that Geertz is more process-centered than product-centered. And this attitude derives from Geertz's ability to see himself and other interpreters more clearly as both inquirers into and subjects of cultural studies.

17. Rorty, "Postmodernist Bourgeois Liberalism," *The Journal of Philosophy* (1983), 583–89, reprinted in Rorty, *Objectivity, Relativism, and Truth;* which also contains his articles "On Ethnocentrism," and "Solidarity or Objectivity?"
18. Geertz, "Anti Anti-Relativism," in Krausz, *Relativism.*

This difference between Geertz and Rorty raises a significant methodological issue. That is, in cultural studies when speaking about "our" view of things and "their" view of things, or when speaking about a "home" interpretation or language and an "alternative" interpretation or language, it seems natural to assume that the "we" and the "they" are determinately characterizable. But, if one adopts the Geertzian view that the cultural interpreter ought to seek self-transformation through his or her studies, by implicating him or her self as a subject of cultural studies, no assumption about the interpreter's determinacy or singularity can be made. So seen, any multiplism of cultural interpretation becomes yet more complex. If interpreters themselves are determinately and singularly characterizable, or if they are not themselves implicated in their objects-of-interpretation, then the locus of multiplism in cultural studies is in the multiplicity of admissible interpretations of an autonomously projected culture. But if interpreters themselves are multiply characterizable, and if they are implicated in their objects-of-interpretation, then the locus of multiplism is to be found in the multiplicity of admissible interpretations of the projected culture *as well as* in the multiplicity of the identities of implicated interpreters. Who is the "us" and who is the "them" becomes an ever more complex and interesting question.

The situation is symmetrical between cultures. Just as we of one culture take different cultural features to be salient, so do agents of alternate cultures. Just as we of one culture are also members of numerous cultures, so persons of alternate cultures may be members of numerous cultures. The subjects, as variously imputed by oneself and by others, exhibit corresponding indeterminacy. So, the boundary conditions of a home culture and an alternative culture may not be determinately fixed. What is internal or external to a given culture may not be clearly delineable. Each is an idealization, both on the part of the interpreter and the native. Yet both the interpreter and the native may still share enough to understand what it might be like to occupy the other's world.[19]

In sum, while critical comparison between interpretations of cul-

---

19. See Nussbaum and Sen, "Internal Criticism."

tures is possible, it is ineliminably tied to one's own culture. Whatever good reasons that can be generated for one's preference for a given interpretation must arise from within one's own culture. Who else's would they be? But since ethnocentrism is ineliminable in this way, there is no access to an overarching metastandard in virtue of which competing interpretations can be conclusively adjudicated.

Part I has been concerned, at the praxial level, to articulate singularism and multiplism as interpretive ideals in the cultural realm. The overriding argument for multiplism has been that, in representative cases, there are no overarching standards with which to adjudicate conclusively between competing interpretations. A contributing argument has been provided by the thesis of imputational interpretation. The reasons for not implicating ontological issues in these praxial considerations will be further developed in Part II.

Part II

INTERPRETATION WITHOUT ONTOLOGY

5
Objects-of-Interpretation and Their Indeterminacy

At several points in Part I, I suggested that a singularist might be tempted to install his or her condition by appealing to practice-independent objects—objects which would be ontologically prior to objects-of-interpretation as constituted within pertinent practices. In Part II, I shall show why such an appeal will not be effective. Briefly, such demonstration will involve showing that the ontological is detachable from the praxial. That exercise, in turn, will involve the claims that singularism is compatible with either ontological realism or ontological constructionism, and that multiplism is compatible with either ontological realism or ontological constructionism. This chapter will be concerned to show how objects-of-interpretation are constituted within interpretive practices, and how differently constituted objects-of-interpretation may be sufficiently self-identical or unicitous for them to answer to competing interpretations. The detachability of the praxial from the ontological will be argued specifically in the case of historical interpretation in Chapter 6. And finally, in Chapter 7, I shall show how ontologically real entities may answer to multiplism. But the discussion of that view should be understood as a thought experiment, and should provide grounds for remaining agnostic with respect to ontological realism as such.

Broadly speaking, we may think of an object-of-interpretation as an intentional object, so construed within a pertinent practice—without presuming, on the one hand, that it is grounded (if possible) in an ontological realism which holds that a real order subsists prior to or behind intentional activity; or, on the other hand, that an object-of-interpretation is grounded (if possible) in an ontological constructionism that positively denies such an order. Rather, I leave open the question of the nature of the relation between putatively practice-independent objects and objects-of-interpretation.

Under one construal, ordinary physical middle-sized objects like sticks and stones are practice-independent. At the same time, some hold that there are very different sorts of objects which also exist independent of particular interpretive practices. These include what may be roughly referred to as Platonic objects. They look like the sorts of idealized entities which Karl Popper says inhabit his World 3, including the objective contents of thought or of works of art or of music, like the structure of a sonata of Bach. They include the sorts of posited structures which ground the invariances of structuralist theories of culture, for example.[1] Having separated these posited "pre"- or "post"-praxial objects from the praxial, I leave open whether one should countenance the existence of such objects or what ontological construal one should place on them.[2] However different ordinary middle-sized objects may be from Platonic objects, they both are understood to be practice-independent, and so I shall treat them in one category on that account.

Commonality or Unicity of Objects-of-Interpretation

Whatever its relation to practice-independent entities, the question of the commonality or unicity of objects-of-interpretation at the

---

1. See, for example, Claude Lévi-Strauss, *Tristes Tropiques* (New York: Atheneum, 1970).

2. A "pan-intentionalist" like Margolis holds that there are no middle-sized entities independently of praxial contexts. In turn, in his Worlds 1 and 3, Popper allows for a distinction between praxial and non-praxial contexts. And, strict behaviorists would deny intentionality altogether, so they would resist the presuppositions of the present inquiry.

praxial level is a function of consensual agreement by pertinent practitioners, based upon good though inevitably local and piecemeal reasons. Singularism and multiplism are adoptable interpretive ideals on the condition that the competing interpretations are about sufficiently common or unicitous objects-of-interpretation, but are not grounded in either an ontological realism or an ontological constructionism. When interpretations impute different properties, they must impute a sufficiently large number of properties in common to warrant the agreement that they are addressing a sufficiently common object-of-interpretation. There is no specific number of properties sufficient for commonality. Whether the clusters of pertinent properties overlap sufficiently is a matter of judgment by informed practitioners. According to the "praxial constructionism" urged here—a constructionism restricted to the level of practice which remains agnostic with respect to ontological matters—an object-of-interpretation is imputable within the constraints of practice. Its identity is not fixed independently of practices as such.

If interpretation involves imputation, and if objects-of-interpretation are interpreted in different ways, it would seem that just the differences in interpretations would mandate differences in objects-of-interpretation. But then how could different interpretations compete at all? They could if they impute *sufficiently* common objects-of-interpretation, ones which are unstable to an allowable degree. Yet, such instability is no unfortunate consequence to be used as part of a reductio argument. Rather, it is a characteristic feature of culturally constituted entities.

Correspondingly, no *particular* properties need to be embodied in an object-of-interpretation for it to be held sufficiently common or unicitous. In imputing objects-of-interpretation, not all properties need be invariant between imputing interpretations. Some interpretations will impute salience to certain properties while disvaluing others as not salient. We allow that objects-of-interpretation may be relatively common with one another while not absolutely so. This condition admits of plasticity over time and over different circumstances of interpretation.

We encountered such commonality when considering the identity of the self in Chapter 3. Specifically, in self-development, one should hold the notion of "self" to be sufficiently plastic so that it might be referred to as that which develops over time and across contexts. Otherwise, if one holds that the initially identified self is not the same as the subsequently identified self, a given self could not have developed. That is, if self-identity were construed absolutely, there could be no such thing as self-development. The concept of self-development would be something of an oxymoron. But it is not. We can refer to one and the same self in the course of its transformation because, again as in Wittgenstein's idea of a cluster concept, there are sufficient, if sliding, properties over time which make possible the re-identification of the sufficiently self-identical entity.

This plastic condition of identity, which Margolis calls "unicity" is exemplified in other cases as well.[3] A river, for example, changes during the course of its geological history. Were one to hold that the river should be absolutely self-identical, any change that it would undergo would result in pluralizing separate rivers. As in the previous case, under such a construal, to say that the river had changed in the course of the last century, for example, would be to utter an oxymoron. But it is not. Where one is right to affirm that an object-of-interpretation is unicitous, the pluralizing maneuver is foiled (See Illustration 4). Whether or not particular objects-of-interpretation are unicitous may well be contestable. Consider further two interpretations of J. S. Bach's Toccata and Fugue. A multiplist might hold that Leopold Stokowski's orchestral rendering of the piece is an ideally admissible interpretation of it, as is that of the original for organ offered by, say, organist E. Power Biggs. But a singularist who deploys the pluralizing maneuver might deny this statement, saying that, however interesting Stokowski's interpretation might be, it is not of an object-of-interpretation sufficiently common with Biggs's. And, on this account, the multiplist and the singularist might not come to agree that the two interpretations compete at all. The two objects-of-interpretation would not have been held to be unicitous. There seems no general procedure to settle the question of when it is appropriate to deploy the pluralizing maneuver.

Without unicitous objects-of-interpretation, interpretations could

---

3. Joseph Margolis, "The Novelty of Marx's Theory of Practice," *Journal for the Theory of Social Behaviour* 19 (December 1989), 367–88.

not compete. But such unicity cannot be absolute, for pertinent interpretations are historically variable. Now, if incongruent interpretations may disagree about which properties are salient, and shifts in previously entrenched agreements affect the stability of objects-of-interpretation, what had been entrenched at one time may cease to be so at another time. So, in the course of such movements, objects-of-interpretation would have no clear boundaries; they would be indeterminate. And the claims about their boundary conditions would be contestable between opposing interpretations.

We have noted that different interpretations may assign salience to different properties when imputing objects-of-interpretation. For example a painting interpreted as part of a series may be thus constituted differently than when it is interpreted as a single work. Specifically, any one of the twelve portraits in Lucas Samaras's *Head Transformation* series may be regarded alone or as part of the series of twelve. There would be no special reason to assign salience, for example, to the subject's right eye in any of these paintings when each painting is regarded alone. But when any of the paintings is regarded in the context of the series, the eye becomes salient just in virtue of the fact that all other discernible aspects of the paintings except this one appear to transform.

In this way, an object-of-interpretation may be variously interpreted so that its properties or its aspects may be said to "reverberate."[4] Aspectual reverberation may be synchronic, as in the the above Samaras example. Or it may be diachronic, as in Van Gogh's *Potato Eaters* when variously interpreted over historical time. In short, such aspectual reverberation need not issue in such instability as to invite the pluralizing of an object-of-interpretation. Aspectual reverberation may issue in an acceptable degree of instability of the object-of-interpretation. And, there is no fixed degree of tolerance in this regard.

Interpretation and Description

An ontological realist might object that if one does not ground objects-of-interpretation in practice-independent objects, one runs the

---

4. I owe the phrase "aspectual reverberation" to David Pears, in conversation.

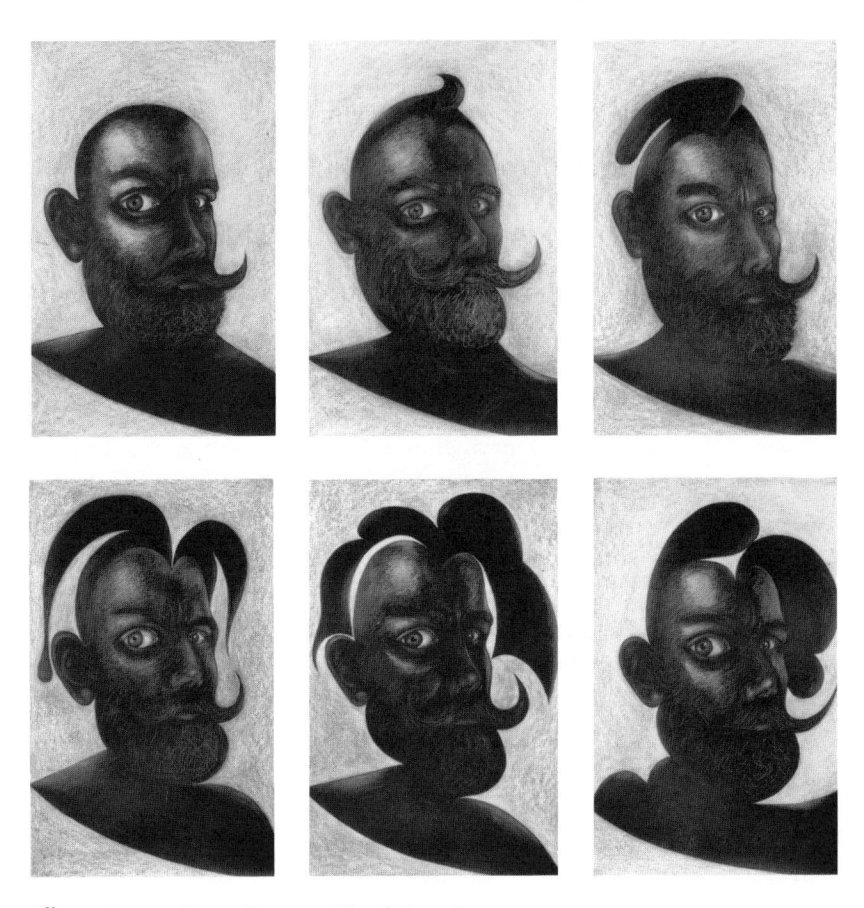

Illustration 10. Lucas Samaras, *Head Transformation* (set of 12), 1982. Courtesy of Pace Gallery, New York

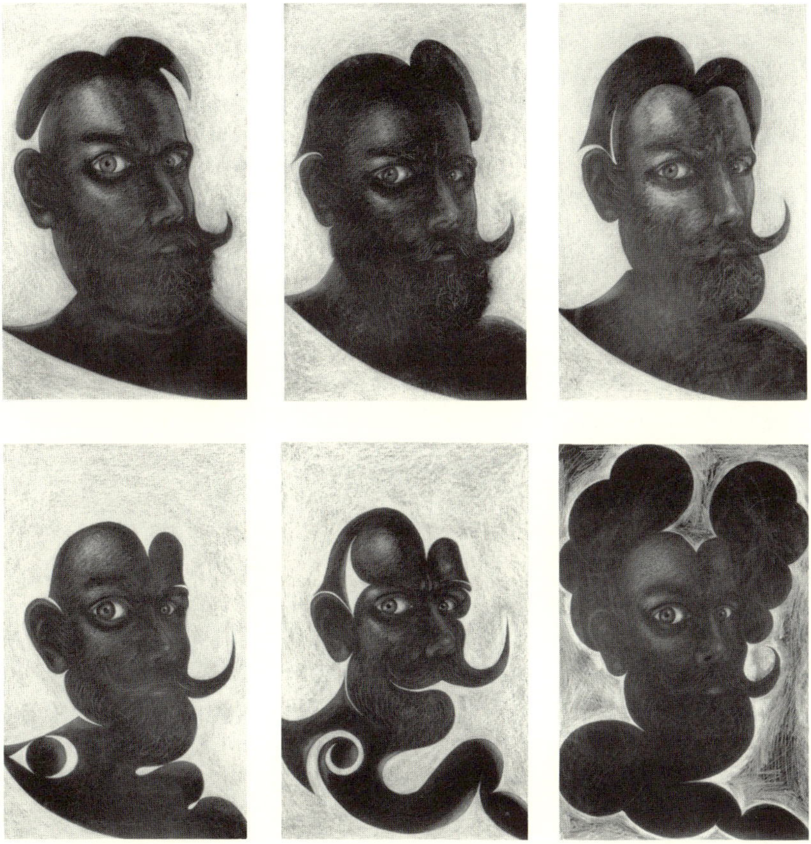

risk of not being able to distinguish interpretation from description. On these grounds, for example, Novitz objects to the view of Margolis. Novitz says that it will not do,

> to distinguish description from interpretation on the basis of the relative stability of their respective objects. According to Joseph Margolis, stable objects are described; unstable ones "whose properties pose something of a puzzle" are interpreted. But the trouble with this, of course, is that our perception of stabilities is itself unstable. How we see the world depends importantly on the beliefs that we bring to perception—so much so that objects are only taken to have certain properties for as long as our beliefs (and theories) about them endure. Since empirical beliefs change, there can be no way of knowing which properties of any object are stable, which unstable. Unless "stability" (and hence "description") is explained in terms of enduring beliefs and knowledge, Margolis runs the risk of reducing all empirical descriptions to interpretations. It is plain, however, that describing cannot be reduced to interpreting. The epistemic structure of the one is manifestly different from that of the other.[5]

But if practice-independent objects are epistemically inaccessible, Novitz's distinction between description and interpretation cannot be put to praxial use. Indeed, rather in the spirit of Nelson Goodman's distinction between facts and conventions, there is no reason why, at the praxial level, we could not embrace a sub-distinction between description and interpretation within the realm of interpretation as such. To say, as Novitz rightly does, that such a distinction would itself be unstable is to recognize what is the case, namely, that in different contexts what is interpretive may be descriptive, and vice versa. Instability of this kind is benign. Further, grounding objects-of-interpretation in practice-independent entities does not eliminate the instability or indeterminacy in question. Alternatively, our praxial constructionism—a constructionism that is limited to the praxial level—holds that requisite stability or determinacy may be insured by the agreement between appropriate interpretations. This agreement

---

5. David Novitz, *Knowledge, Fiction, and Imagination* (Philadelphia: Temple University Press, 1987), p. 95.

is to be consensually sanctioned by pertinent practitioners, who are constrained in their turn by the rationality of the reconstructions of the tradition in which the objects-of-interpretation appear.

Benign Instability and Indeterminacy

There is no need to eliminate fully the instability or indeterminacy of cultural objects-of-interpretation. Consider the question in literature, for example. In a characteristic passage, E. D. Hirsch says

> meaning is an affair of consciousness not of words. Almost any word sequence can, under the conventions of language, legitimately represent more than one complex of meaning. A word sequence means nothing in particular until someone either means something by it or understands something from it. There is no magic land of meanings outside human consciousness. Whenever meaning is connected to words, a person is making the connection, and the particular meanings he lends to them are never the only legitimate ones under the norms and conventions of his language.
> One proof that the conventions of language can sponsor different meanings from the same sequence of words resides in the fact that interpreters can and do disagree. When these disagreements occur how are they resolved? Under the theory of semantic autonomy they cannot be resolved, since the meaning is not what the author meant, but "what the poem means to different sensitive readers." One interpretation is as valid as another, so long as it is "sensitive" or "plausible."[6]

Hirsch's argument is reconstructable as follows: (1) conventions of language can sponsor different meanings; (2) such multiplicity is to be eliminated by fixing upon particular meanings as willed by particular persons; (3) meaning is an affair of consciousness of words; and, (4) without so fixing meanings, we face, as he says, a "chaotic democracy of readings."

The first statement of the reconstructed argument is correct. Con-

---

6. E. D. Hirsch, Jr., *Validity in Interpretation* (New Haven: Yale University Press, 1967), pp. 3–5.

ventions of language *can* sponsor different meanings. But the second statement is misguided. Hirsch presupposes without argument that all interpretive disagreement should end with full convergence. There is no reason why this should be so. Hirsch also presumes that *particular* persons, rather than communities of interpreters or language users, are required for fixing meanings. Thus, Hirsch's equation of consciousness with individual consciousness is mistaken. The second statement assumes that when particular persons do fix meanings they may not simultaneously fix different meanings allowable by the conventions of language. Finally, the fourth statement just does not follow from the premises. Allowing that there may be a multiplicity of meanings does not entail that there must be a "chaotic democracy of readings." Multiplicity of meanings may allow for constraints on the range of ideally admissible meanings.

Hirsch's argument arises from a rejection of indeterminacy of meaning in literature. Let us then identify our understanding of this notion. I assume one of the definitions provided in the *Oxford English Dictionary* (1961): "...not of fixed extent, number, character or nature...." This definition does not understand indeterminacy in terms of an epistemic lack. Correspondingly, I do not understand indeterminacy in objects-of-interpretation in terms of epistemic lack, according to which the object-of-interpretation would be determinate but there would be some barrier to our knowing its putative determinate nature.

But Hirsch favors a different view:

> Reproducibility is a quality of verbal meaning that makes interpretation possible: if meaning were not reproducible, it could not be actualized by someone else and therefore could not be understood or interpreted. Determinacy, on the other hand, is a quality of meaning required in order that there be something to reproduce. Determinacy is a necessary attribute of any shareable meaning, since an indeterminacy cannot be shared: if a meaning were indeterminate, it would have no boundaries, no self-identity, and therefore could have no identity with a meaning entertained by someone else.[7]

---

7. Ibid., pp. 44–45.

Hirsch is right to require reproducibility and shareability for interpretation. But he is wrong to say that indeterminate meaning cannot fulfill these conditions. After all, "clouds" and "species" have indeterminate extensions but one shares them perfectly well. Hirsch's mistake deflects him from examining an interesting avenue of inquiry which leads him to embrace the false doctrine that indeterminate meaning could have *no* boundaries, *no* self-identity, *no* identity shareable by different people. Surely the distinction between determinate and indeterminate is a matter of degree. So it would be best to speak of meaning as being more or less determinate rather than determinate or not. These terms are comparative rather than absolute.

Hirsch's confusion can be seen in this passage: "Determinacy, then, first of all means self-identity. This is the minimum requirement for shareability. Without it neither communication nor validity in interpretation would be possible."[8]

Hirsch assumes that self-identity must be absolute. I have suggested, contrariwise, that indeterminacy (or sufficient determinacy) may satisfy the requirement of sufficient self-identity or unicity. As Margolis says:

> nothing could be referentially fixed that did not exhibit a certain stability of nature; but how alterable (or by what means altered) the life of a person or the restored *Last Supper* or the oft-interpreted *Hamlet* or the theoretically intriguing *Fountain* or the marvelously elastic *Sarrasine* may be is *not* a matter that can be decided, or that is actually determined merely, by fixing such texts or artworks *as* the reidentifiable referents they are.[9]

In other words, objects-of-interpretation need not be determinate in Hirsch's absolute sense. Indeterminate meanings may indeed be sufficiently determinate and self-identical for requisite interpretive purposes.

Hirsch affirms that an individual will is required to fix meaning if it is to be determinate in his sense. And this requirement leads him

---

8. Ibid., p. 45.
9. Margolis, "Reinterpreting Interpretation," *Journal of Aesthetics and Art Criticism* 47 (Summer 1989), 241–42.

to his defense of authorial meaning as capturing *the* meaning of a work. But, as I have averred, nowhere does Hirsch seriously consider the social intentionality of meanings. He mistakenly thinks that the rejection of the theory of semantic autonomy automatically commits him to the view that meaning must be fixed by individual persons.

To reiterate, Hirsch urges us to fix putatively singular meanings of texts in order to avoid the "anarchy" of multiplism. To do so, he urges us to retrieve the intentions of the creator. Now, besides the epistemological difficulties of access to those intentions, the meaning(s) of texts simply are not stable in the way Hirsch presumes—stable, that is, over the contexts of interpretation in which either the original creator(s) or receiver(s) may operate. That is, with the recontextualization of the text, the object-of-interpretation is open to various interpretations. This sort of shifting accounts for the instability of the object-of-interpretation, and makes the Hirschian program of fixing the determinate meanings of texts—which he takes to be invariant between interpretive contexts—quite impossible. In sum, there is no possibility nor is there a need to eliminate fully the instability or indeterminacy of cultural object-of-interpretation.

So far in this discussion I have been speaking of an object-of-interpretation being indeterminate in that it admits of no clear boundaries. I have assumed this sense of indeterminacy in my discussion of Novitz and Hirsch, for example. There is a distinct second sense of indeterminacy which pertains directly to the thesis of multiplism. According to it an object-of-interpretation does not uniquely determine its interpretation; it underdetermines its interpretation. In Chapter 7 I shall indicate how indeterminacy in the first sense bears on indeterminacy in the second sense. Specifically, an object-of-interpretation may be so indeterminate in the first sense that it gives rise to the indeterminacy of interpretations in the second sense. Yet not all indeterminate (in the first sense) objects-of-interpretation need result in indeterminacy in the second sense. This issue will be developed further when I consider the general thesis of the detachability of praxial ideality from ontology. But first we should consider the specific case of historical interpretation where that thesis is exemplified.

6

Historical Interpretation without Ontology

To articulate more fully the detachability of ideality from ontology, let us now consider how an ontological realist, an ontological constructionist, and a praxial constructionist might theorize about the nature of historical inquiry. Their strategies, which are replicable in other cultural practices, are exemplified with particular clarity in this case.

Ontological Realism and Ontological Constructionism in History

The ontological realist says that history is about real past actuality. The ontological constructionist says that history cannot be about a past actuality but rather it is about what survives the materials and procedures of historical research. Both of these views may well accede to a praxial constructionism, according to which, in the actual conduct of historical inquiry, a historian is constrained by what survives the materials and procedures of historical research, whether or not there is a real or intelligible past actuality.

With respect to the historical past, consider the thesis of ontological constructionism urged by Leon Goldstein and compare it with the ontological realism urged by Patrick Nowell-Smith.[1] Nowell-Smith puts the contrast in this way:

> *The Realist Thesis.* The historian's aim is to discover and tell us what actually happened at certain times and places in the past; historians succeed in this, at least sometimes.
> *The Constructionist Thesis.* History is what the evidence compels us to believe.[2]

Nowell-Smith's characterizations needs some adjustment, since a realist might well agree that the product of historical research is what the evidence compels one to believe. So, we might strengthen his characterization of what I have called the ontological constructionist thesis by suggesting that, in addition to its claims about specific beliefs, the ontological constructionist thesis further denies that history is about a past actuality.

Now, in defence of a "global" ontological constructionism, Goldstein says: "the referents of historical statements or statements of memory are not to be found outside of the framework of knowing. There is no way to reach outside such frameworks; the knowing situation is not compatible with such a reaching out; both the statements which refer and the objects to which they refer are constituted within the framework of the investigation. There is no epistemic way, as distinct from conceptual word-play, to reach out from within that framework to realistic objects."[3]

Goldstein says further: "At no point does nature break into our consciousness—if that makes any sense—to present itself unmediated by the methodologies of knowing. Choices are made, theories are accepted and disregarded, thinkers and theorists come to definite conclusions as to the character of natural reality, and no verbal sleight of hand about reasoning truly brings the unmediated into account."[4]

Goldstein's constructionism in history is a special case of his global

---

1. Leon Goldstein, *Historical Knowing* (Austin: University of Texas Press, 1976); and "History and the Primacy of Knowing," *History and Theory* 16 (1977).
2. Patrick Nowell-Smith, "The Constructionist Theory of History," *History and Theory* 16 (1977), p. 1.
3. Goldstein, "History and the Primary of Knowing," p. 40.
4. Ibid., p. 47.

constructionism, according to which we can have no knowledge of a reality independent of the framework of knowing, for the objects of knowledge "are constituted within the framework of the investigation." He wants his "remarks to be general," since he believes that "the primacy of knowing is a generally sound epistemological stance," though he does not want "to stray too far from philosophy of history."[5]

We should note that if one were to deny global ontological constructionism, ontological constructionism in history would not on those grounds have been disallowed. In piecemeal fashion, one could be an ontological realist with respect to ordinary middle-sized objects, for example, and still be an ontological constructionist with respect to history. Ontological constructionism with respect to particular practices does not depend upon global ontological constructionism.

I have characterized Goldstein's view as ontological constructionist insofar as he denies the intelligibility of historical referents that lie outside the framework of knowing. He not only holds that we may not have epistemic access to such referents, but also considers the very idea of such referents unintelligible. Yet one could agree with the thesis that historical referents, realistically construed, are epistemically inaccessible, and still affirm that—as a matter of transcendental or second-order theory—there must be such objects in virtue of which one could explain the coherence of what is epistemically accessible. In short, as in science (for example, according to the view of Karl Popper), one may well be an ontological realist and not tie that claim to the further claim that one may indeed have epistemic access to the putatively real referents.[6] And, according to the argument, such realism can provide the grounds for an account of reference and truth.

Goldstein, however, seems to reason that if referents outside the framework of knowing are epistemically inaccessible, it follows that ontological realism of any sort is wrong.

> If there is anything to be said for the view that the truth or falsity of a claim to knowledge is determined by the character of its re-

---

5. Ibid.
6. Karl R. Popper, *Realism and the Aim of Science* (Totowa, N.J.: Rowman and Littlefield, 1983).

ferent, and if in history there is no referent except as it is constituted or constructed by means of the techniques of historical investigation—which is the point of my saying that in history the distinction between fact and the assertion of fact does not exist... then it is hard to see how reference in history can be achieved by a reaching out from within the framework of knowing to the facts and events of an unmediated real past. Put another way, if the reference of an assertion is determined by attending to what is looked for by those who are qualified to determine its truth, the realist view of the matter seems to have little in its favor.[7]

Goldstein seeks to block a "non-access" realism by suggesting that the idea of referents outside the framework of knowing is "factually vacuous." Thus, any account of reference or truth that presupposes such an idea is correspondingly "factually vacuous."

At the same time, when Goldstein gears his remarks to the epistemology rather than the ontology of history, he seems to leave open the possibility of a non-access realism—never mind that the latter could do no epistemological work. For example, he says: "This is what I mean when I say that the real past cannot serve as the touchstone for the truth of historian's claims. It does not seem to enter into the work of historical investigation at any point."[8]

Surely a non-access realist might well agree that the real past cannot serve as the touchstone for the truth of historian's claims in the sense that the real past, insofar as it is epistemologically inaccessible, could not help the historian to sort out which competing historical statements should be accepted or rejected. Such sorting would indeed remain within the framework of historical knowing. In that sense the real past, the non-access realist could agree, does not seem to enter into historical investigation.

In turn, Nowell-Smith concedes that we can have no access to the real past against which historical interpretations may be tested. And he holds that our inability to gain access to past reality lies in its not being present, which is a rather different point from Goldstein's general claim that mediation precludes epistemic accessibility. But, sep-

7. Goldstein, "History and the Primary of Knowing," p. 51.
8. Ibid., p. 35.

arate grounds aside, both writers agree that the real past is inaccessible.

Yet, Nowell-Smith holds that there *is* room, if nonepistemological, for the idea of a real historical past. And the work that such an idea should do is precisely the philosophical work that helps to make sense of the very idea of historical reference and truth. Along these lines Nowell-Smith distinguishes between *extreme realism* and *less extreme realism* in history, rejecting the former and embracing the latter.

> [T]he discipline of history as it is actually practiced, is at no point dependent on the observation or even the possibility of observation of past events. We can take the inaccessibility of past events to present observation as a datum, and once this is granted the extreme realist is immediately refuted.
>
> But the less extreme realist... is committed only to the thesis that if an historian states truly that such and such happened, it happened whether or not anyone found out that it happened or proved by constructionist methods that it must have happened. Caesar's crossing the Rubicon is the sort of event that can be observed and no doubt was observed when it happened, but the less extreme realist thesis is not limited to events of the observable kind. If Schneider really showed that urban oligarchy was transformed into a landowning aristocracy in the period from 1219 to 1324, then this transformation is something that actually happened, a slice of the real past, even though it was not, when it occurred, something which anyone could have 'observed' or with which anyone could have been 'acquainted' in the philosophical sense of those words which Goldstein adopts. This less extreme realism is just as much at odds as is its more extreme brother with Goldstein's idea that historians construct events, with his distinction between the real and the historical past, and with his assertion that the real past has no role to play in the historian's enterprise, since the less extreme realist holds that the historian constructs an account of the real past—the only past there was—and that the real past plays the important role of being that to which statements, when true, refer.[9]

In short, Nowell-Smith's less extreme realism attempts to account for the idea of historical truth; namely, without presuming epistemic

---

9. Nowell-Smith, "The Constructionist Theory of History," pp. 6–7.

access to the historical past, historical claims refer to a practice-independent reality. Such a practice-independent reality may include items that are directly observable at the time of their occurrence, such as Caesar's crossing of the Rubicon. Or, being abstract, such entities as urban oligarchy or landowning aristocracy may not have been directly observable at the time. In either case, according to Nowell-Smith, the historical referent is not something that the historian constructs.

Goldstein might object to this point by suggesting that abstract historical entities are not simply *given* at the time of their putative occurrence. Rather, they were constructed or postulated perhaps by thinkers contemporary with the event. This possibility, in turn, raises the question whether historical persons are abstract entities, and whether they should be understood along constructionist lines.

Nowell-Smith worries that the constructionist's construal of historical persons as such will not do. As he says:

> if we say, with the constructionist, that Caesar's crossing the Rubicon is constituted by the historian in the course of his research, it is easy to slip into thinking that the Caesar referred to in the historian's text is also a "constructed" or, as it is sometimes put, a "postulated" or "theoretical" entity whose ontological status is, or is like, that of electrons. It is easy to slip into this way of talking since Caesar himself has been inaccessible to observation for a long time, so that the argument which the constructionist uses to show that his crossing the Rubicon is a constructed event applies with the same force to show that Caesar himself is a constructed person.[10]

But Goldstein disagrees. Recognizing that the person standing in front of somebody is President Jimmy Carter hangs on praxially constituted procedures of knowing, including the constructed concept of President of the United States. To say that one is actually observing such a person is not, contrary to Nowell-Smith's impulse, to say that such a construction is fictive. Generally, then, on Goldstein's view, if the idea of a real historical past can do no methodological work, it should be dropped. And, in virtue of its failure to do methodological

---

10. Ibid., p. 12.

work, we should say that the past just is what praxial procedures lead us to believe.

On my view this claim is too strong. Although the idea of a real past can do no methodological work, it may do philosophical work. Having said this, however, one may well remain *agnostic* and make no choice between the ontological realist and ontological constructionist accounts of the historical referents. The praxial and the ontological concerns are logically detachable. Recall our distinction between ontological constructionism and praxial constructionism. The ontological constructionist holds to the thesis that there is no past beyond that constructed by historians. Not only would a putative past actuality be praxially otiose, but the truth conditions of pertinent historical claims *could not* reside in such a past actuality. On the other hand, the praxial constructionist makes no claim about whether there is a past actuality beyond that constructed by historians. He or she affirms only that if there were such a past it could do no praxial work. In saying that "what the historian constructs is not just a theory or account of what happened, but *the events themselves*," Goldstein embraces the ontological constructionist position.[11]

On the other hand, Nowell-Smith holds that, irrespective of epistemic access, truth conditions of historical statements reside in past actuality. Nowell-Smith diagnoses Goldstein's view in the following way:

> It is Goldstein's assimilation of questions of the form 'Is p true?' to questions of the form 'How do you know that p?' and his use of the notion of a 'touchstone of truth' which straddles the two senses of "verification" that leads him to the distinction between the real and the historical past, with all the difficulties that that distinction brings with it, and to the assertion that the real past has no role to play in historical construction. For if the only role that the real past could play was that of being the touchstone of truth in the sense that statements about the past cannot be known to us unless what they state is directly observed, that would be rather obviously true. But what Goldstein has not shown is that the real past cannot be that to which historical statements refer.[12]

11. Goldstein, "History and the Primary of Knowing," p. 5.
12. Nowell-Smith, "The Constructionist Theory of History," p. 19.

Goldstein embraces the ontological constructionist view that there *are* no objects beyond constructed objects-of-interpretation. But, as I say, his claim is too strong. He could have remained agnostic about any putative objects beyond constructed objects-of-interpretation. It would have been enough had he embraced a praxial constructionism, which would have captured his correct motivating insight that all that is pertinent to the practice of history lies at the methodological or the praxial level. He should have stopped there.

We need not agree with Goldstein's view that it is philosophically (rather than methodologically) vacuous to embrace an ontological realism in order to agree with him that, at the praxial level, all that is at hand is what is praxially constructed. Indeed, the ways in which both the historian who embraces ontological constructionism and the historian who embraces ontological realism proceed with their practice are, on that account, indistinguishable. In regard to practice, one can embrace either or neither ontological theory about the relation between the historical past and the actual past.

It is interesting to note that we may draw this same general conclusion when we deploy the rather different idiom of E. H. Carr.[13] His view is a kind of hybrid between Nowell-Smith's and Goldstein's. It captures both Nowell-Smith's assertion of the real past and Goldstein's constructionist view of the historical past. And it does not render past actuality "factually vacuous." Unlike Goldstein, who construes the historical past constructionistically and holds the idea of past actuality to be factually vacuous, Carr draws a distinction between *basic facts* (which are those facts that capture past states of affairs but are not as such objects of historical interpretation) and *historical facts* (which are those facts historians regard as pertinent to an historical interpretation).

> These so-called basic facts, which are the same for all historians, commonly belong to the category of the raw materials of the historian rather than of history itself.... [T]he necessity to establish these basic facts rests not on any quality in the facts themselves, but on an *a priori* decision of the historian.... The facts speak only when the historian calls on them: it is he who decides to which

13. E. H. Carr, *What Is History?*, 2d ed. (Harmondsworth: Penguin Books, 1987).

facts to give the floor, and in what order or context. It was, I think, one of Pirandello's characters who said that a fact is like a sack—it won't stand up till you've put something in it.... It is the historian who has decided for his own reasons that Caesar crossing that petty stream, the Rubicon, is a fact of history, whereas the crossing of the Rubicon by millions of other people before or since interests nobody at all.[14]

Carr observes generally that "the belief in a hard core of historical facts, existing objectively and independently of the interpretation of the historian, is a preposterous fallacy, but one which is hard to eradicate."[15]

For Carr, both basic facts and historical facts are mediated. But from this observation Carr does not conclude (unlike Goldstein) that realism—even of basic facts—is disallowed. Carr construes basic facts realistically. He emphasizes that historical facts are the proper domain of history, while basic facts are not. Basic facts constrain historical facts; they are the "materials" out of which historical facts are constructed. Historical facts are historically interpreted basic facts. Since interpretation is part and parcel of historical practice, basic facts are not part of the domain of history properly understood.

Carr's construction of historical facts concerns their selection from the pool of basic facts, based on conditions of relevance provided by pertinent interpretations. It is in this sense that basic facts are the raw materials of history, and not in the sense that they are unmediated, or inchoate, or anything of the sort. Interpretations bestow significance or salience upon basic facts. Correspondingly, several interpretations may agree or disagree about which basic facts should be identified as historical facts.

So, while Goldstein is a constructionist with respect to all facts, Nowell-Smith is a less extreme realist with respect to Carr's basic facts, and Nowell-Smith allows a constructionism with respect to Carr's historical facts. In turn, Carr is a realist with respect to his basic facts and a constructionist with respect to his historical facts. It is revealing to note that all three thinkers agree to a constructionist

14. Ibid., p. 11.
15. Ibid., p. 12.

construal of Carr's historical facts, which are facts so constituted at the praxial level. In my terms, they agree to the praxial constructionism of historical objects-of-interpretation.

The agreement by Nowell-Smith, Goldstein, and Carr about praxial constructionism brings to mind our discussion in Chapter 5 about the distinction between descriptions and interpretations or, as Nelson Goodman would say, the distinction between facts and conventions. The distinction between descriptions and interpretations may be itself embedded in interpretive practices. For example, in history, while an ontological realist may say that basic facts contrast with historical facts in that the first are described and the second are interpreted, the ontological constructionist may say that what are initially taken as basic facts are also interpreted but that they may function in different ways in different practices. The ontological constructionist may allow the distinction between basic facts and historical facts, but construe it differently than the ontological realist. Following Carr's idiom, the ontological constructionist in history could say that it is not just historical facts that are interpreted, for basic facts are interpreted as well. It is rather that basic facts are those that are not interpreted *for historical purposes:* they are not taken by practitioners of history as historical objects-of-interpretation. But that is not to say either that they are not interpreted or that they may not be taken by some other practice as appropriate objects-of-interpretation.

For example, that Caesar crossed the Rubicon is a historical fact and that, for all we know, he ate five small meals a day is not. This is to say that Caesar's crossing of the Rubicon, when and as he did, constituted a violation of Republican law which had profound historical significance. And his eating five small meals a day had no corresponding historical significance. But, in turn, with respect to an alternative practice like Roman gastronomy, Caesar's custom of having five small meals a day could well count, in a parallel way, as a significant "anthropological fact," and with respect to such a practice his crossing of the Rubicon would recede as a mere basic fact.

So seen, the distinction between facts and interpretations becomes a matter of use in a given practice. Correspondingly, the often cited motto, "it's interpretation all the way down" may be taken in either of two ways. It may be taken (more strongly) by the ontological constructionist as amounting to the claim that *there is nothing* autonomous of interpretation as such, or (more weakly) by the praxial constructionist that with respect to a pertinent practice there is nothing other than objects-of-interpretation. Again, I remain agnostic on the stronger construal and embrace the weaker.

To adopt Nelson Goodman's parallel talk of facts and conventions, we may agree with him that all convention in interpretive practices depends upon fact, "yet all fact is convention."[16] Insofar as the distinction between facts and conventions is a matter of practice, we may agree with Goodman when he synopsizes his view as follows:

> In sum, I have been arguing such obvious points as that there is no firm distinction between fact and convention, but that that distinction is very important; that the line between fact and convention shifts often and may be drawn anywhere but is not capricious; that when a convention (as option) becomes a convention (as the usual), it thus tends to become factual; and that rather than the facts determining how we take them, how we take them determines the facts—but that we had better be careful how we take them.[17]

My only emendation to Goodman's remarks is a matter of emphasis. "How we take them"—facts and conventions—is a function of the practices in which they operate.

To summarize, the ontological realist and the ontological constructionist may agree that at the praxial level objects-of-interpretation are the products of construction. They disagree, however, about the explanation of the coherence of objects-of-interpretation. But one need not engage in the controversy about what explains such coherence in order to address the question of praxial ideality, for the former question does not settle the latter question.

We may note in passing that multiplism in history, as generally conceived, is itself multiplied in such special kinds of history as the history of art and history of religion, where objects-of-interpretation

---

16. Nelson Goodman, "Just the Facts, Ma'am!" in Michael Krausz, ed., *Relativism: Interpretation and Confrontation* (Notre Dame: Notre Dame University Press, 1989), p. 81.
17. Ibid., p. 85.

are judged to be significant according to a multiplicity of contending evaluative standards. For example, the idea of the history of art involves judgments about what is authentically to be taken as art as opposed to non-art. The idea of the history of religion involves judgments about what is authentically to be taken as religious as opposed to non-religious. These are histories whose objects-of-interpretation are taken to be "authentic" according to some standard of values. What is taken as artistic or religious partly constitutes the subject matter and serves as a criterion for selecting the historical facts. Indeed, histories of art and religion reflect the very contentiousness of these notions. But one might suggest that the problem of grounding these second-order views of authentic art and religion arise again. That is, it might be urged that the distinction between authentic art and non-art or between authentic religiosity and non-religiosity requires some grounding beyond the merely praxial. Without something beyond the merely praxial, it might be urged, these distinctions cannot be made out. Yet again—perhaps especially paradoxical in the case of the history of religion—no ontological grounding is mandated. One may well understand pertinent criteria in praxial constructionist terms, and at the same time remain agnostic about any putative ontological grounding. Praxial constructionism does not require any particular ontological grounding.

Praxial Constructionism and Pragmatism in History

In regard to the present discussion of historical interpretation, the pragmatist's general attitude is pertinent. According to it, one should not ground claims of historical truth or falsity in a theory of the real, whether ontological realist or ontological constructionist. Yet, in the absence of such a theory, one need not refrain from holding that such statements are true or false. That is, holding certain statements to be true or false does not presume that one should have a theory of truth or falsity, or a theory of the ontology of the objects which constitute their truth conditions.

Further, the pragmatist holds that it is precisely on the ontological realist hypothesis that the distinction between the real past and the historical past can be drawn to start with; that without an ontological realist hypothesis no such distinction can be drawn. Put otherwise, the historical past is distinguished *in opposition to* the real past. So seen, the differences between Nowell-Smith and Goldstein arise only after the distinction is granted. And, given that there is a distinction between the real past and the historical past as Nowell-Smith draws it, it is no wonder that Nowell-Smith should charge Goldstein with "idealism." Should that distinction not be granted, the discussion between Nowell-Smith and Goldstein would amount to a pseudodebate.

The pragmatist might press the view that any distinction between ontological realism (again, the view that there are real objects beyond the praxial level) and ontological constructionism (the view that there are no objects beyond the praxial level) is itself suspect, for drawing such a distinction presumes a kind of ontological realism in the first place. The praxial should not be understood *in opposition to* any ontologically real objects, affirmed or denied. The praxial should not be understood in terms of an ontological theory of any sort. So, the pragmatist eschews both the ontological realist and the ontological constructionist view insofar as they make any ontological claim at all. Rather, the pragmatist holds that the praxial should be understood fully in terms that pertain to an historically constituted practice. That is all.[18] If, for example, one were to distinguish between the historical past and past actuality—the former being a construction of the practice of history and the latter being that to which such constructions putatively refer—and, if one would then claim that the latter was factually or philosophically vacuous (as Goldstein does), still too much would have been conceded to ontological realism. For the pragmatist, the distinction between the ontological and the praxial could not be made out if the idea of the praxial is understood *in opposition to* the ontological.

Yet one might hold that there is a perfectly good distinction to be drawn between the real past and the historical past, and that this distinction does answer the need to separate historical claims from

18. See, for example, Richard Rorty, "Solidarity or Objectivity?" in Krausz, *Relativism*.

other sorts of claims, such as anthropological or scientific claims. The distinction between the real past and the historical past would not, however, coincide with the distinction between nonconstructed and constructed. Rather, both pasts would be constructed. If this much is conceded, the charge of idealism would have no sting, for praxial constructionism would not entail idealism. Idealism affirms that the real is exhaustively captured by the mental. Although idealism is compatible with praxial constructionism, a praxial constructionist might agree or disagree with a mentalist construal of the historical past. So, on this view, Goldstein was not sufficiently constructionist with respect to the real past, in contrast to which he offered his constructionist view of the historical past. He conceded too much to the realist by assuming that the real past should be understood to be not constructed.

One may, therefore, remain quite agnostic about any presumed ontological backdrop—not just in the sense that one makes no claim about the nature of an order beyond the praxial, but in the further sense that one makes no claim about the very intelligibility of such an order. In turn, although the ontological has not been deployed, the way is open to formulating a praxial understanding of objects-of-interpretation. Even if one rejects the distinction between ontological realism and ontological constructionism (or for that matter the distinction between practice-independent objects and objects-of-interpretation) one may embrace a *praxial constructionism,* according to which, innocuously, statements about objects-of-interpretation are made intelligible within the terms of pertinent practices.

The point can be extended. It might be urged that the claim that praxial ideality is detachable from the ontology of cultural entities depends upon a distinction between objects-of-interpretation—taken as such within the context of a practice—and putative practice-independent objects. Now, while a pragmatist may be sympathetic with seeing the ontological drop out, he or she may have some doubt about the distinction just drawn. For example, in order to resist any distinction that is analogous to the one between scheme and content (and this one is), Donald Davidson might hold that the idea of an objects-of-interpretation in opposition to a putative practice-independent object is indefensible.[19] It would replicate something like the distinction between scheme and content.

But the idea of an object-of-interpretation—whether or not in opposition to the idea of a practice-independent object—*can* be defended, since the former does not presuppose the intelligibility of the latter. All that is required is that objects-of-interpretation are what interpretations are about within the context of practices. Whether there is anything at all beyond practices, or anything that is intelligible beyond practices, need not be of concern. It is not so much that the coherence of the idea of an object-of-interpretation depends upon the coherence of the idea of a practice-independent object. Rather, affirming the coherence of the idea of an object-of-interpretation serves to distinguish it from what a realistically inclined theorist might urge as a real constituent of the world, whether or not that latter notion is intelligible at all.

When one considers the cases of music, art, and culture, for example, the very idea of a practice-independent object might initially have appeared odd, in that the issue of the detachability of ideality from ontology might have been thought to have arisen from a view that was not coherently adoptable. But we have seen that, particularly in the case of history, the ontological realist's position is no straw man's, and that in its light we can see how the ontological realist's position with respect to the other cases considered could be formulated if not here embraced. And we can see how a praxial constructionism can be formulated independently of a presumption of ontological realism.

Let us now turn directly to the issue of the detachability of ideality from ontology, and further consider the question of the indeterminacy of objects-of-interpretation.

19. Donald Davidson, "On the Very Idea of a Conceptual Scheme," in Jack Meiland and Krausz, eds., *Relativism: Cognitive and Moral* (Notre Dame: Notre Dame University Press, 1982); and Davidson, "The Myth of the Subjective," in Krausz, *Relativism*.

7

Praxial Ideality without Ontological Realism

Let us now collect several themes that have been suggested in previous chapters. I have remained agnostic about whether the very idea of a practice-independent object in cultural practices is coherent. The ontological realist affirms that it is; the ontological constructionist affirms that it is not; the praxial constructionist leaves the matter open. Yet, even if the idea of practice-independent objects in cultural practices is coherent, there is no way to inspect such objects. They can do no praxial work.

Further, as we shall see, ontological realism as such does not require complete determinacy of its objects. Indeed, depending upon the degree of indeterminacy, an object may answer to either one or several ideally admissible interpretations. And, where the indeterminacy of an object is attenuated, it may be appropriate to pluralize it. This may be a step toward installing a singularist condition. Where the indeterminacy of an object is not attenuated, it may not be appropriate to pluralize it. This may be a step toward a multiplist condition.

In any case, cultural and noncultural practice-independent objects need not be assumed to be completely determinate for either singularist or multiplist conditions to obtain. An ontological realist could be a multiplist on the condition that the practice-independent object is sufficiently indeterminate that it would answer to multiple ideally admissible interpretations. For example, an ontological realist construal of a work of music may allow that Muti's and Comissiona's interpretations are both admissible on the grounds that the ontologically real work is sufficiently indeterminate to answer to both. This possibility suggests the logical compatibility of ontological realism with multiplism, and it constitutes part of the argument for the detachability of ideality from ontology. Given that the ontological realist's would-be objects are not accessible, however, the question of the compatibility of ontological realism and multiplism is scholastic from the praxial constructionist's point of view.

Before expanding upon these themes let us enumerate several points of strategy. First, in regard to our thesis of the detachability of praxial questions from ontological questions, we should reiterate our special usage of "ontological" and the views that fall under it, namely "ontological realism" and "ontological constructionism." "Ontological" here ranges over the theses of ontological realism and ontological constructionism. That is all. Ontological realism and ontological constructionism as construed in this book are mutually exclusive and comprehensive of the ontological field. Of course, one could still imagine alternative characterizations of the ontological in which such exclusivity and comprehensiveness do not obtain.[1] If, for example, one were to ramify the field of the ontological in other terms, the thesis of logical detachability would have to be adjusted accordingly. Yet I have not inventoried the many senses of realism and constructionism in currency in the philosophical literature. Indeed, they are legion and nonconvergent.[2] Consequently, the remark that imputational interpretation, for example, might commit one to a distinct ontology in some other sense would be benign in regard to the present thesis.

---

1. See, for example, Joseph Margolis, *The Truth about Relativism* (Oxford: Basil Blackwell, 1991); he argues for a kind of realism and constructionism of cultural entities *within* a historicist or praxial framework. Synoptically, we may say that Margolis embraces the theses of (1) cognitive intransparency, (2) the historicity of thinking, (3) the symbiosis of subject and object, and (4) the social constructionism of the self. Taken together, they suggest that there is no first philosophy. These themes lead to the general conclusion that there is no unique solution to interesting philosophical issues.

2. For some formulations of realism, for example, see Hilary Putnam, *Meaning and the Moral Sciences* (London: Routledge and Kegan Paul, 1978), pp. 20–22; Michael Devitt, *Realism and Truth* (Princeton: Princeton University Press, 1984), pp. 34–35; and Rom Harré, *Varieties of Realism* (Oxford: Basil Blackwell, 1986).

Second, it might be suggested that the ontological realist is a straw man in that no one seriously holds the view that there are practice-independent objects in cultural practices; that, for example, there are practice-independent musical works, art works, past actualities, or culturally "naked men" (to use an unfortunately gendered phrase of Stuart Hampshire). That is, even considering ontological realism as a candidate position for grounding questions of ideality is misplaced. But we may observe that ontological realism with respect to such cultural entities is well represented, whether it is for Popper in regard to musical and artistic works or Nowell-Smith in regard to history, or Levi-Strauss and other structuralists in regard to human nature.[3] In turn, ontological realism with respect to middle-sized objects is rather commonly represented—whether by naive realists or by not-so-naive realists such as Karl Popper, Nicholas Rescher, or E. M. Zemach. Such representation is significant for our purposes as we keep in mind the singularist strategy which mandates that when singularism appears to be foiled one should expand the field of discussion to include areas that neighbor the cultural domain in question; and these areas might well include the domain of middle-sized objects. The ontological realist position in history (either extreme or less extreme) as characterized by Nowell-Smith, for example, is of this kind. So seen, the ontological realist position is by no means unrepresented or inconsequential.

Third, we should recall the distinction between *piecemeal* realisms or constructionisms and *global* realisms or constructionisms. The piecemeal realists and constructionists apply their claims over particular practices. The global realists and constructionists apply their claims over the entire field of practices. Thus, for a particular practice, while global realists and constructionists would have to oppose each other, piecemeal realists and constructionists would not. For example, ontological realism or ontological constructionism in music does not

---

3. Of course, one might say that the appeal to an ontological realist view of musical works, for example, is implausible in the face of the idea that musical works cannot exist as such independently of notation, and that notation is praxially constituted. While I agree with this point, that does not preclude the temptation to idealize such notationally constituted entities into non-notated entities. Recall such a temptation in Grossman and more extremely in Wolterstorff.

entail ontological realism or ontological constructionism in history, and so forth. Clearly, the absence of an argument for global ontological realism or ontological constructionism does not preclude the possibility of a piecemeal ontological realism or ontological constructionism.

Fourth, if we keep in mind Alexander Nehamas's singularist-constructionist view about the postulated author, it is easier to show that ontological realism is not required for singularism than that ontological realism is compatible with either singularism or multiplism.

Fifth, the ontological realist does not understand objects-of-interpretation to be ineliminably seen under specifiable historical and cultural conditions. For him or her, its terms transcend such contexts. The object-of-interpretation is an entity posited through a *via negativa* by subtracting what seem to be terms specific to appropriate practices. For example, although Popper concedes that works of music are brought into existence in certain historical and cultural circumstances, he holds that in their creation they transcend such circumstances to inhabit a world that is autonomous of any particular historical or cultural setting. Popper holds that such entities exist independent of interpretation practices. Morris Grossman and Nicholas Wolterstorff hold similar views in regard to music, as does Nowell-Smith in regard to past actuality.[4] But it remains a mystery what properties the putative practice-independent objects could have. If there is no way to find out, the very idea of a practice-independent object, if intelligible, could do no praxial work. For both the ontological and praxial constructionist, on the other hand, objects-of-interpretation are ineliminably praxial, always to be seen in certain specifiable historical and cultural circumstances. They are not about anything that might exist autonomously of them. Whatever—if anything—might lie "behind" or "above" or "beneath" them is otiose.

Sixth, the ontological realist could well agree that objects-of-interpretation at the praxial level might be constructed. In this he or

---

4. Morris Grossman, "Performance and Obligation," in Philip Alperson, ed., *What Is Music?* (New York: Haven, 1987); Nicholas Wolterstorff, "The Work of Making a Work of Music," in Alperson, *What Is Music?;* and Patrick Nowell-Smith, "The Constructionist Theory of History," *History and Theory* 16 (1977).

she could agree with the ontological constructionist. As we saw in the case of history in Chapter 6, both ontological realism and ontological constructionism may agree with praxial constructionism. Correspondingly, the idea of an object-of-interpretation is ontologically neutral. It is agreeable to both the ontological realist and to the ontological constructionist.

Seventh, I have adopted the term "indeterminate" rather than "vague," since indeterminacy suggests a feature of a thing, while vagueness suggests a feature of one's understanding or perception of that thing. Throughout this discussion indeterminacy has been used as a feature of a thing—either a practice-independent object (for the realist) or an object-of-interpretation (for a praxial constructionist)—rather than as a feature of one's understanding or perception of it. To say that some things are indeterminate does not violate the law of self-identity: that to be something it must be identical with itself, and not another thing. There is no reason to believe that an indeterminate object could not be identical with itself. Clouds, for example, are indeterminate and self-identical.

The Very Idea of Practice-Independent Objects

The ontological realist takes the idea of practice-independent cultural objects to be coherent, while the ontological constructionist does not. In turn, the praxial constructionist remains agnostic on the point. The ontological realist may be tempted to ground or make determinate objects-of-interpretation by tying them to putatively practice-independent objects. But, for the ontological constructionist, objects-of-interpretation cannot be grounded in this way, since practice-independent objects are not only epistemically inaccessible but the very idea of such objects is incoherent. Yet, an ontological realist like Nowell-Smith may concede that putative practice-independent objects are epistemically inaccessible and so practice-independent objects could not ground or make determinate objects-of-interpretation. He nevertheless posits such practice-independent objects as a transcendental or second-order *explanation* of the nature of objects-of-interpretation. That is, they provide a way of talking altogether about reference. More generally, the ontological realist need not presume epistemic access to practice-independent objects to use the idea of such objects as the basis for a transcendental or second-order account of the ideas of reference or the growth of knowledge, for example. Still, the ontological realist who concedes the epistemic inaccessibility of practice-independent objects cannot use such an idea as a way to ground or make determinate objects-of-interpretation. Under these conditions, while the idea of practice-independent objects might be used in a transcendental or second-order account of reference or the growth of knowledge, it cannot be put to praxial use in grounding particular objects-of-interpretation.[5] In contrast, constructionists (either ontological or praxial) would have to account for such ideas as reference or the growth of knowledge along very different lines.

Yet ontological realist David Novitz, for example, insists that one may indeed have epistemic access to practice-independent objects. His argument appears to address both middle-sized and cultural objects. Novitz claims to have identified a fallacy characteristically committed by those who oppose such epistemic access. He calls it the "Occlusive Fallacy."

> The fallacy takes the following form. It is supposed, first of all, that our experience of X, where X is the world and its objects, can be explained in terms of a favored entity or process Y. From this it is inferred that we really experience only Y, and that X is no more than an inference from, or a construction of, Y. Ys are believed to form a veil, a barrier, between experiencing subjects and the Xs that were previously considered to be the bona fide objects of their experience; and sometimes the Ys even come to be regarded as the ultimate constituents of reality.
>
> The fallacy is obvious. It involves accepting the explanation of what it is to experience the world in order to show that we do not,

---

5. This point is made by Karl Popper himself in his theory of verisimilitude, when he characterizes his realism as metaphysical. See his *Conjectures and Refutations* (London: Routledge and Kegan Paul, 1963), as well as his *Realism and the Aim of Science* (Tofowa, N.J.: Rowman and Littlefield, 1983). Other ontological realists who concede no direct access to a practice-independent order include Ian Jarvie, *Rationality and Relativism* (London: Routledge and Kegan Paul, 1984); Nicholas Rescher, *Scientific Realism* (Dordrecht: Reidel, 1987); Devitt, *Realism and Truth;* and, of course, Nowell-Smith, "The Constructionist Theory of History."

after all, experience the world—and hence in order to reject the explanation on which this conclusion is based. Put yet more plainly, the rejection of the explanation presupposes its acceptance. If the invocation of Y really is an adequate explanation of our experience of X, then Y or Ying is just what it is to experience X. If, on the other hand, we do not really experience Xs, so that our invocation of Y is not an explanation of what it is to experience X, then there is no need to take the invocation of Y—the "explanation"—seriously, and *a fortiori* no need at all to regard Y as the sole object of our experience.[6]

Notice that even if Novitz's argument was in the end sound, his realism would not thereby have been established; a nonrealist argument would only have been shown faulty. And even if realism with respect to middle-sized objects could be successfully defended, that would not entail a realism with respect to cultural entities.

But is Novitz's so-called occlusive fallacy a fallacy at all? Novitz begins his reconstruction of the nonrealist's argument (here I call it a "nonrealist" rather than an "antirealist" argument to allow for agnosticism) by suggesting that Y explains our knowledge of the world and its objects. But, in the first instance, the world and its objects need not be construed in the realist way that Novitz chooses; one may well remain neutral with respect to their ontological construal. Indeed, the construal of the world and its objects is just what is at issue. It is also an open question whether Y is, in the sense pressed by Novitz, a proper *explanation* of X at all. So, in order not to beg the question from the start, the construal of "the world and its objects" needs to be left ontologically neutral. There is no fallacy if one does not construe the world and its objects in an ontologically realist way. Given Novitz's question-begging construal of the world and its objects, he would have been right to have identified a fallacy. But it was he who pinned the fallacy on to the nonrealist.

However indefensible may be the appeal to practice-independent objects in order to ground middle-sized objects-of-interpretation, it becomes even less plausible in the case of cultural entities. As our

---

6. David Novitz, *Knowledge, Fiction, and Imagination* (Philadelphia: Temple University Press, 1987), pp. 56–57.

discussion of the musical case has shown, it is only in relation to pertinent practices that an interpreter can justify claims of interpretive admissibility. Any questions about the determinacy or indeterminacy of putatively practice-independent cultural objects, if coherent, would be scholastic.

Joanna Hodge reinforces the point when she says:

> Music... and indeed art in general, is often taken to reproduce, represent, or express some occult humanity, or occult value, which is produced in some other domain, and then transposed into publicly accessible form, in sentences, or music, or artworks. However, not only has this reference back to an occult domain absolutely no explanatory power, since the explanation is offered in terms of a domain which remains, inevitably, occult. It further substitutes for and blocks off the possibility of beginning to give an account of what is actually in process in the production of meaningful language, the composition of music, and more generally in the production of artworks. Appeal to a meaning and value transcending the medium in which they are articulated is a barrier to understanding, and functions as a central myth, both assigning value to art and philosophy, and disempowering them from any substantive contribution to understanding what it is to be human.[7]

Indeed, no putatively practice-independent cultural objects are required. Praxial procedures are enough.

Indeterminacy in Language

At the praxial level there is an inherent indeterminacy in the very language in which objects-of-interpretation are cast. For any general predicate there will always be a more determinate predicate that could be applied. For example, one may begin with a general statement and

---

7. Joanna Hodge, "Aesthetic Decomposition: Music, Identity, and Time," in Michael Krausz, ed., *The Interpretation of Music: Philosophical Essays* (Oxford: Clarendon Press, 1993), 250.

then make it more determinate by unpacking its implied ellipses. The statement, "The sea is rough" is general and invites unpacking its ellipses answering such questions as: roughness for whom, and for what purposes? If we say that the sea is rough for sailing by an intermediate sailor, for example, we might be pressed to unpack our understanding of intermediate. To this we might respond that the sailor of intermediate skill is someone who is neither a beginner nor advanced. But the distinctions between beginner, intermediate, and advanced are themselves indeterminate. There are no clear boundaries between these terms. So, we may say that determinacy is relativized to which contrasting term a given term is compared. Indeed, it might be better to drop an absolute distinction between determinate and indeterminate and replace it with a comparative distinction between more or less determinate or, still better, between more or less indeterminate.

In turn, consider the case of a painting with a brownish-redish patch. In attributing brownishness or reddishness to the patch there will always be some further discrimination that one could make—that it is perhaps red oxide or burnt sienna. To say that it is brownish-reddish is not to say what the determinate color it. Here the object-of-interpretation may be indeterminate relative to the more determinate designations: red oxide or burnt sienna. Yet there remains an open-ended indeterminacy here as well, since we might ask, whose red oxide or whose burnt sienna—that of Grumbacher or Permanent Pigment or some other pigment manufacturer? It is well known among artists that such pigments from different manufacturers do not exactly match one another. And there is no procedure for stipulating which should be the definitive color. There is no bedrock of absolute determinacy. Even stipulation has built into its ellipses the indeterminacies of language and language users as such. Again, the degree of determinacy or indeterminacy for each term is relative to the contrasting term with which it is being compared.

Yet, given the pertinent ellipses in these cases, it remains singularly true or false that the sea is rough or that the color patch is reddish-brown. Therefore, an indeterminate object-of-interpretation may well answer to a singularist requirement. Absolute determinacy of objects-of-interpretation is not necessary for a singularist condition, since a single ideally admissible interpretation may apply to indeterminate objects-of-interpretation. Correspondingly, the multiplist condition is not mandated simply by the fact of indeterminacy.

Yet, an object-of-interpretation may be so indeterminate that on that account a multiplist condition would obtain. Recall our discussion in Chapter 3 of F. W. Bateson's and Cleanth Brooks' interpretations of Wordsworth's Lucy poem. Whatever the work is—a realistic and practice-independent existent or a praxially constituted or imputed object-of-interpretation—it is sufficiently indeterminate to be able to answer to these competing interpretations. The same holds for the competing interpretations of Beethoven's First Symphony, and for the competing interpretations of Van Gogh's *Potato Eaters*. The multiplist may allow such incongruent interpretations on the condition of the relative indeterminacy of pertinent objects-of-interpretation.

Constraining Objects-of-Interpretation

Consider that work of music referred to as Bach's Toccata and Fugue, for example, which is taken to be unicitous with respect to such diverse interpretations as those offered by conductor Leopold Stokowski and organist E. Power Biggs. For argumentative purposes let us assume with Novitz that we may have access to pertinent practice-independent objects. The question arises whether they could ground or make determinate the objects-of-interpretation. On the assumption of accessibility, it would seem that practice-independent objects could make objects-of-interpretation (more) determinate if the practice-independent objects were more determinate than the pertinent objects-of-interpretation initially were. And this would be so even if the practice-independent object were not fully determinate.

One might remark that by suggesting that indeterminate practice-independent objects might (on the realist's account) constrain the range of ideally admissible interpretations I have contradicted my claim that ideality is logically detachable from the ontology of middle-sized or cultural entities. But the claim that putatively practice-independent objects—even if indeterminate—might (on the realist's account) constrain the range of ideally admissible interpretations is not tantamount to the claim that they may determine whether a singularist or a multiplist condition obtains. And this is what is at issue.

This thought should be placed in the context of three concerns: putative practice-independent objects, objects-of-interpretation, and interpretations. Certain objects-of-interpretation may answer to a multiplist condition because the object-of-interpretation is so indeterminate that it would be unclear which one of the competing interpretations it would answer to. The singularist, in attempting to establish a one-to-one correspondence between interpretation and object-of-interpretation, would then seek to eliminate or sufficiently minimize the indeterminacy. If the singularist is also an "access" ontological realist he or she might be tempted to eliminate or minimize such indeterminacy by appealing to the ontologically real (and presumably the relatively more determinate) object to which the object-of-interpretation is tied. By so doing, the indeterminacy of the object-of-interpretation could be appropriately adjusted.

But the nature of the pertinent tie between practice-independent objects and objects-of-interpretation remains obscure. If we concede further the possibility that a more determinate practice-independent object could ground or make more determinate an object-of-interpretation, how might this be done? We may see this difficulty in the context of an example in which, in order to dismantle a multiplist condition, a singularist might attempt to make an object-of-interpretation more determinate by appealing to a putative practice-independent object.

Recall our discussion in Chapter 3 of the multiplicity of interpretations of Van Gogh's *Potato Eaters*. There the object-of-interpretation was indeterminate. For the formalist interpretation, the object-of-interpretation was thought to have been exhausted by elements internal to the painting. And for the psychological, Marxist, and feminist interpretations, the object-of-interpretation was more widely construed to include, respectively, the psychological, economic, and gender conditions embodied in the painting but not bounded by it. The interpretations were taken as competing, on the condition that the objects-of-interpretation in question were unicitous with one another. But, as discussed, a singularist might wish to establish a singularist condition by pluralizing the initially unicitous object-of-interpretation, that is, by separating out more determinate objects-of-interpretation from what was initially thought to have been a less determinate object-of-interpretation. This option is open, and its appropriateness is an essentially contestable matter, subject to the reasoned judgment of informed practitioners.

But there appears to be no pre-existent practice-independent object to which to appeal—however determinate or indeterminate. And even if there were such an object, how one might find and inspect it remains altogether obscure. Further, even if one allowed the introduction of practice-independent objects to reduce indeterminacy in objects-of-interpretation, there is no reason to believe that those practice-independent objects would be themselves sufficiently free from indeterminacy.

Ontological Indeterminacy of Practice-Independent Objects

Let us pursue the question of the indeterminacy of practice-independent objects in its own terms, even though the issue of their deployment remains scholastic for the praxial constructionist. As I say, one motivation that singularists might have to ground or make determinate objects-of-interpretation by appeal to putative practice-independent objects might arise from their assumption that such objects would be determinate, and that such determinacy is required for singularism. But the inclination to ground or make determinate objects-of-interpretation by tying them to practice-independent objects is lessened when—aside from the fact that determinacy of objects-of-interpretation is not required for singularism—it is recognized that ontological realism itself does not require that practice-independent objects be fully determinate. Again, there is no bedrock of determinacy. Indeed, according to ontological realist E. M. Zemach, practice-independent objects are characteristically indeterminate.

Consider the thought that practice-independent objects may be indeterminate, now focusing on middle-sized objects. One might theorize that the range of ideally admissible interpretations of middle-sized objects may be narrowed to a limit of one on the assumptions at least that, (a) there are practice-independent objects (as the ontological realist holds); (b) one has epistemic access to middle-sized objects; and (c) such objects are determinate, that is, they have clear boundaries. Clearly one can be an ontological realist and embrace (a) and (b) without embracing (c). That is, one can be an ontological realist and leave open whether the pertinent practice-independent objects are determinate or indeterminate.

As a thought experiment, let us concede (a) and (b) but not (c). Determinacy of practice-independent objects is not a necessary condition for singularism. Further, indeterminate practice-independent objects may answer to either singularism or multiplism. The indeterminacy of objects-of-interpretation is compatible with either singularism or multiplism. Whether singularism or multiplism obtains is a function of the match between the relative indeterminacies of pertinent objects-of-interpretation and their interpretations. Correspondingly, if one were to endorse an ontological realist position (a) and (b), it would be plausible to hold that practice-independent objects may constrain the range of ideally admissible interpretations, but there is no guarantee that it should constrain the range to a limit of one. Put otherwise, limited determinacy of objects-of-interpretation may constrain the range of admissible interpretations, but limited determinacy does not mandate singularism.

To expand upon our thought experiment, let us consider Zemach's discussion of the indeterminacy of practice-independent objects. He accepts (a) and (b) but not (c). Zemach is a global ontological realist for whom practice-independent objects are epistemically accessible. At the same time, he holds that such objects are characteristically indeterminate.[8] Zemach holds that reality is what it is, no matter what anyone thinks of it or how it is interpreted. Yet, ontologically, objects are characteristically indeterminate. "[T]he thesis of ontological determinacy of all objects is incorrect. I do not deny that ontologically complete objects exist, and that the concept of absolute Leibnizian

---

8. See E. M. Zemach, "In Defense of Relative Identity," *Philosophical Studies* 26 (1974), 207–18; "Schematic Objects and Relative Identity," *Nous* 16 (1982), 295–305; "No Identification without Evaluation," *British Journal of Aesthetics* 26 (Summer 1986); see also Zemach's *Types* (Leiden: E. J. Brill, 1992).

identity applies to them. But... the overwhelming majority of the objects actually referred to, objects such as Jimmy Carter, this shirt, the man on my right, etc., are *not* ontologically complete. The concept of identity which applies to them is not absolute identity."⁹

More fully, Zemach argues as follows:

> Let me assume now the thesis which I wish to refute, i.e., that every object is ontologically complete. In this case it will turn out that the overwhelming majority (perhaps all) of the singular terms used in any human language denote nothing at all. The reason is this: a fully determinate entity must have clearly defined boundaries; otherwise it would be indeterminate whether certain features belong to it or not. But no name or definite description used in our language denotes an entity whose boundaries are sharply defined.

According to Zemach, the description 'man on my right' does not determine to which ontologically complete entity it applies. While it applies to the one who exists upon birth, birth itself is a lengthy process and no one of its stages may be taken as determinately fixed. The entity denoted by 'the man on my right' is further indeterminate in that it answers to the one who started to exist at birth or at conception or somewhere in between. Such indeterminacy also obtains at the temporal end-point of the entity denoted. The concept 'man' does not specify when the entity ceases to exist, that is, when the heart stops, when brain activity stops, or, in the case of the 'dead man', how much the skeleton should not turn to powder before it is a man no longer. On the assumption of ontological determinacy, if the heart stopped before brain activity ceased, one would have two distinct entities, the one with a terminal point later than the other. In response to such an anomaly Zemach concludes that one cannot specify the exact boundaries of every entity to which we refer. Nevertheless, we may indeed refer to them. The alternative is unacceptable. "If we accept the assumption that every object we can refer to is ontologically complete we must conclude that all singular terms fail to refer."¹⁰

---

9. Zemach, "Schematic Objects and Relative Identity," 295.
10. Ibid., 296–97.

Zemach's argument suggests that ontological realism is not automatically committed to the determinacy of its objects. Since the indeterminacy of objects accommodates either singularist or multiplist conditions, Zemach's realism allows for the possibility of the heterodox view that makes ontological realism and multiplism compatible. (See Illustration 1.) While the indeterminacy of practice-independent objects allows for the multiple interpretability of its objects, it does not entail such interpretability. As we saw, indeterminate objects could answer to singularist conditions.

Although Zemach's realism is compatible with his observation that definite descriptions are characteristically incomplete, that observation is neutral with respect to whether there actually are practice-independent objects. Put otherwise, the incompleteness of definite descriptions does not entail the existence or nonexistence of practice-independent objects. An independent argument to establish such existence would be required. Zemach's argument for the indeterminacy of practice-independent objects does not actually show such objects to be practice-independent. He only assumes that they are. Indeed, a (ontological or praxial) constructionist could actually embrace Zemach's argument to the effect that characteristically one cannot specify determinate boundary conditions of an object-of-interpretation. As mentioned, the constructionist could well argue that the indeterminacy of objects-of-interpretation arises as a feature of the indeterminacy of the language. Yet, the constructionist does not take the fact of the indeterminacy of language as an invitation to assert that there are practice-independent objects or that they are either determinate or indeterminate. In this way, a constructionist might embrace Zemach's treatment of the indeterminacy of language while either denying or remaining agnostic about the existence of practice-independent objects.

Zemach's argument shows that ontological realism does not require practice-independent objects to be determinate. There is no need to require absolute determinacy for middle-sized objects nor, we may add, is there reason to require it for cultural entities. Whatever the case may be with respect to middle-sized objects, the question of the determinacy of practice-independent objects does not arise for the praxial constructionist. Such objects can do no praxial work. This is especially so in the cultural realm. Given the issues of intelligibility and access to putatively practice-independent objects in the cultural realm, they could not function to constrain the range of ideally admissible interpretations.

But for an ontological realist a cultural entity may be so indeterminate that on that account a multiplist condition could obtain. For example, for the ontological realist, the dispute between F. W. Bateson's and Cleanth Brooks's interpretations of Wordworth's Lucy poem is possible on the condition that the poem is unicitous (and so indeterminate), and that the poem answers to both interpretations. For the ontological realist this would also be the case for competing interpretations of musical works: Muti's and Comissiona's interpretations of Beethoven's First Symphony, for example, would be understood to be about a unicitous real entity sufficiently indeterminate to answer to both interpretations. In turn, the ontological realist would offer a similar view of visual art works: the formalist, psychological, Marxist, and feminist interpretations of Van Gogh's *Potato Eaters* would be seen as competing interpretations of an autonomous and practice-independent entity which is unicitous and so indeterminate that it could answer to these interpretations. An ontological realist would offer a similar gloss on historical events, and other cultural entities.

In any event, quite apart from the question of determinacy, the praxial constructionist holds that it is otiose to deploy practice-independent objects to settle questions of ideality. Let us now review our results.

Conclusion

I have said that one may be a singularist and either an ontological realist or an ontological constructionist. Or one may be a multiplist and either an ontological realist or an ontological constructionist. Put otherwise, singularism entails neither ontological realism nor ontological constructionism; and multiplism entails neither ontological realism nor ontological constructionism. (See Illustration 1.) The question of ideality is logically detachable from the question of ontology.

The combination of the singularist and the ontological realist is rather orthodox; such a realism characteristically assumes that a real entity answers to a unique interpretation (as Popper does). The combination of multiplist and ontological constructionist is also rather orthodox; such a constructionism characteristically assumes that its objects-of-interpretation are constructed and that they answer to a multiplicity of interpretations (as Goldstein does). More heterodox but self consistent are the remaining combinations. One may be a singularist and an ontological constructionist by denying that there are any ontologically real entities and by further requiring that interpretive constructions should pursue a single right interpretation (as Nehemas does). Finally, one may embrace the heterodox multiplist and ontological realist view by holding that there are ontologically real entities and they may answer to multiple interpretations (as Zemach does).

I have not embraced ontological realism nor, for that matter, ontological constructionism. The point of showing that one may self-consistently hold to such views is to constitute part of the argument that ideality and ontology are logically detachable. Consequently, as regards ideality, one may remain agnostic with respect to ontological realism or ontological constructionism. Put otherwise, if one were an ontological realist one would not on that account be a singularist. And, if one were an ontological constructionist, one would not on that account be a multiplist. But I do not embrace ontological realism—not so much because it is false (it may not be false, especially as regards middle-sized objects), but because one does not need it in the case of praxial ideality of cultural entities. Praxial constructionism is enough.

Correspondingly, whether or not there is such a thing as, for example, a "historical order" independent of pertinent interpretive practices does not enter into an effort to settle whether the range of ideal interpretations is singular or multiple. Whether or not there is such a thing as, for example, a history "as it actually was," or whether there are any plausible analogues to it in the other considered cultural practices, are questions that do not need to be resolved in order to settle whether the range of interpretations should be singular or multiple. To be singularist or multiplist with respect to these areas does not require a prior commitment to ontological realism or to ontological constructionism. Thus, while Goldstein discounts the intelligibility of a past actuality and therefore embraces an ontological constructionism, I remain agnostic about the ontological claim. I thereby allow that Nowell-Smith's less extreme realism might be coherently formulable, holding with Nowell-Smith that his less extreme realism, whatever other work it might do, could do no praxial work. Indeed, whether or not ontological realism is coherently formulable, I have restricted my concern to the question of praxial ideality.

In turn, multiplism would obtain where, for competing interpretations about a unicitous object-of-interpretation, there are no overarching standards to adjudicate between such interpretations. In the case of Beethoven's First Symphony, we saw how a musical score underdetermines its interpretation. Two competing interpretations may be of a unicitous object-of-interpretation, and each is justifiable according to different plausible standards. Yet no overarching standard is available with which to rank pertinent interpretations conclusively. In the case of Van Gogh's *Potato Eaters,* we saw how objects-of-interpretation underdetermine their interpretations, and how different incongruous interpretations are applicable to a unicitous object-of-interpretation. In history, we saw that basic facts underdetermine historical objects-of-interpretation and their interpretations. Whatever the ontological construal one places on basic facts, the question of the range of ideally admissible interpretations at the praxial level is logically detachable. We saw how there may be no neutral and overarching standards in virtue of which personal programs may be conclusively ranked, and how they might be mutually incongruous. Yet each might be justified in its own terms. In the case of alternative cultures, we saw how the object-of-interpretation is praxially constructed from the home culture, including the projection of a home culture's "us" and an alternative culture's "them." So no overarching standard between pertinent interpretations is culturally neutral.

I have suggested that whichever praxial ideal one should embrace for a given practice depends upon the consensus of informed practitioners, constrained by the rationality of the reconstructions of the traditions from which pertinent objects-of-interpretation arise. Such a decision depends, in part, upon answers to such questions as whether a given object-of-interpretation or a given interpretation should be pluralized or aggregated.

In my discussion of the critical comparability of interpretations whose standards are incommensurable, I indicated both that there is a logical space for inconclusive reasons for preferences, and that such reasons are characteristically not so strong as to embody standards that would conclusively adjudicate between the pertinent interpretations. They might embody general values or guidelines for the reasonableness, appropriateness, or aptness of interpretations, but they would be too weak to count as adjudicating standards.

On the generally Kantian assumption that legitimate philosophical explanations should be necessary or universal, one might challenge my piecemeal approach by suggesting that it does not constitute a genuinely philosophical explanation. But such an assumption is precisely what is called into question by this book. There is no reason to privilege necessity or universality as a requirement for philosophical explanation. Indeed, the historicist stance of this book suggests an alternative view of what a philosophical account could be.

What of the rightness of this present account? If there may be inumerable interpretations of interpretation, the question of its unicity would have to be taken up by appropriately constrained informed practitioners. Under these circumstances it would be an open question whether interpretation would be sufficiently unicitous with the object-of-interpretation of this study. That is, whether this interpretation of interpretation and yet another may genuinely compete depends upon whether its objects-of-interpretation are unicitous, and that is something for subsequent investigations to determine.

In any case, if one were to argue that the interpretation of cultural interpretation does after all answer to a singularist condition, one would not thereby undercut the general thesis argued here, since the present account does not entail that the practice of interpreting interpretation must be one of the characteristic cultural practices that are multiplist. I leave open whether the interpretation of interpretation should be one of those cases that might unseat the universal claim of singularism.

I have avoided speaking of truth or falsity rather than admissibility and inadmissibility for two reasons. First, I have been concerned with interpretation as it ranges over a number of different kinds of practices, including some for whose interpretations it would be strained to say they are true or false. For example, it would be strained to say that one musical interpretation was true or false in anything but an attenuated sense, and in any case that sense of truth and falsity would need to be unpacked in ways similar to those I have used to unpack admissibility and inadmissibility. Second, to substitute truth and falsity (in the usual bivalent sense) for admissibility and inadmissibility would invite begging the question about key logical issues concerned with admissibility and inadmissibility. Alternatively, one would need to unpack truth and falsity in a non-usual sense, which in turn would amount to an effort similar to that which I have attempted here for admissibility and inadmissibility.

While my general stance has been anti-essentialist and anti-foundationalist as regards objects-of-interpretation in the cultural realm, I have set aside the question whether middle-sized objects or objects of the formal and natural sciences should be understood as cultural objects. Yet, the present discussion bears on the question of the differences between cultural and noncultural practices, since now, at least, singularism cannot be taken as a sine qua non of rationality and so should not be adopted as a universal aim. It opens the way to consider to what extent singularism and multiplism might distinguish the cultural from the noncultural realms.

Consequently, the present discussion may serve as something of a prolegomenon to a comparative study of a full range of practices. On a piecemeal basis, one might ask whether the interpretations of middle-sized objects, objects of the formal and natural sciences, and objects of cultural studies are characteristically singularist or multiplist; whether anything like an ontological realism may be rightly employed to make their objects-of-interpretation more determinate; and whether either their indeterminacies are better understood in terms of their relation to practice-independent objects or in terms of their praxial constructions. These sorts of questions may be asked in a comprehensive comparative account of a fuller range of practices. Whatever one finally concludes about singularism and multiplism in cultural practices, the chief purpose of this book will have been served if it has provided useful terms and strategies with which to pursue such questions.

Appendix
From an Interview with a Luo Medicineman

Consider the following excerpt from an interview I conducted in Nairobi on February 6, 1985 with Tago Athieno, a Luo medicineman. My informant, Odera Oruka, translated and commented. Tago began the interview by chanting for about five minutes, accompanying himself on two indigenously crafted rattles. After showing me other instruments—including small drums and single- and double-stringed instruments made of rudimentary materials—Tago agreed to answer questions.

TA: You cannot teach someone to be a witchdoctor. It comes to you spiritually. But there are people who think they can become witchdoctors by just trying—that they can learn and they try, but then they don't become good ones. Those are the ones who deceive. They don't have the calling....

If you are spiritually possessed you go to the witchdoctor. If it's a physical illness, you go to the hospital.... But the witchdoctor cures physical illness too. There is no conflict between hospital medicine and witchcraft. There is no real conflict. There are certain things that are clear-cut and can be cured by a medical doctor, like malaria. But there are other illnesses which can be cured only by a witchdoctor. Like, for example, some moral sin. For example, incest. You cannot be cured by a doctor in hospital. But it is still a moral sin, and it can haunt you and cause damages. You can be cured by a witchdoctor.

MK: Then a sin is understood as a disease. Is that right?

TA: Yes, something like that. But the "disease" is wider. It covers whatever you feel.

MK: Suppose somebody committed incest. What would be an appropriate treatment? What would be the witchdoctor's treatment?

TA: In that case, you kill a lamb, take its blood, and go to where the thing took place. Take a bit of the sand or something, and mix these. Sprinkle this on the victim. And if possible, let him sit a bit. He can wash himself. The victim is to be made conscious all the time that he is being cured of incest.

MK: Who would be the victim, the person who did it or the one who received it?

TA: The one who received it. But the one who did it did the sin. And he can be cured of his sin.

MK: Now, what is to be cured here? Is it that the one who commits incest becomes possessed? Is that what one wants to get rid of?

OO: He [Tago] says this thing has gone into this man's heart. There is a translation problem here. Sometimes by "heart" they also mean something that is in the mind. So that physically you feel pain. So in a way there may be both a physical and mental effect. When he says that someone is cured, he says that cure is both the physical and the mental.

MK: Can you say what is wrong with incest?

TA: Once a man is going with his daughter, having sexual relations with her, once you do that kind of thing it goes into your heart, it goes into your mind. That kind of moral wrong-doing goes into your mind. Because you have done something abominable in the community . . . that it must bother your mind forever. That will, of course, cause a lot of other harm in you, which will appear physically. Like being so indifferent to whatever is going on around you in the community. Like becoming thin. Like being useless as a social producer.

MK: What makes it bad? Is it bad because it causes us to be possessed, or are we possessed because it is bad?

TA: In addition to that—apart from its making you possessed—it also hastens your death.

MK: Is there another reason why it is bad, besides its making you possessed and its hastening your death? Is there also another reason, for example, is it because God said so?

TA: Another reason is that it is bad for the community. The community condemns it. It is bad—even if you don't care about the fact that you are possessed.

MK: Why is it bad for the community?

TA: The community must condemn him. It is doing something which is never done. That is forbidden. It is bad for the community. If he does it it can destroy the community.

MK: You have been talking about incest. Do you think this is the worst sin? Or, which are the worst sins?

TA: You see, incest is a "Kira," which covers all kinds of things. But it is not the whole thing. Kira covers all worst moral sins.... There is also another form of sickness... that somebody has done... yes... if someone interferes with your fate somehow. That is another form of sickness. Someone is jealous of your progress or something, and does certain things which will insure that you end up very unsuccessful. That is also a Kira.

MK: Now in incest we have been talking about relations between a man and a woman. What about the relations between a woman and a woman, and between a man and a man? What about homosexual relations? Are such relations allowed?

TA: No. That is bad. That is another kind of Kira. That is an example of a bigger sin like incest and interfering with someone's fate. It is in the same category.

MK: What is destructive about such relations?

TA: It is something out of the blue. It is unthinkable. It is so rare and abnormal. It is not easy to see how one could justify it. It is very bad for the community....

Index

Aggregating strategy, 56–60
Ambiguity, 69
Anarchy, 49–53, 96–97, 130
Arben, David, 19
Aristotle, 5
Aspectual reverberation, 123
Athieno, Tago, 89, 167–69
Authentic music movement, 2, 23

Bach, Johann Sebastian, 14, 18, 35, 56, 122
Bateson, F. W., 78–79
Beardsley, Monroe, 2, 48, 63
Beethoven, Ludwig van, 19, 20–21, 35, 51, 52
Behaviorism, 120n.2
Biggs, E. Power, 122
Booth, Wayne, 41
Bremmer, H. P., 70, 72, 74, 77
Briskman, Larry, 82–84
Brooks, Cleanth, 78, 79
Brusilow, Anshel, 23
Buddhism, 91n.33

Carnap, Rudolf, 2
Carr, E. H., 138–40
Christianity, 34
Cluster concept, 122
Collective creation, 47

Collingwood, R. G., 102
Comissiona, Sergiu, 21, 103, 104, 147
Commonality, 55–56, 120–23
Computer music, 17
Conceptual schemes, 61–62
Conclusivity, 21–22, 30, 50, 101–5. *See also* Standards
Constructionism, 5. *See also* Ontological realism and constructionism; Praxial constructionism
Critical monism, 41–42
Critical pluralism, 41–42
Cultural myths, 100–101
Cultural objects-of-interpretation: aggregation of, 56–60; choice of terminology, 39n.2; commonality/unicity of, 55–56, 120–23, 156–57, 163–64; constraints on, 155–57; context of, 13–18, 32; as defined by interpretation, 68–69, 77, 93–95, 97; distinction from interpretation, 98; emergent qualities of, 23, 48; and formalism, 70, 72; historical constitution of, 2, 95–96, 98, 100–101, 149; incompleteness of, 13–18, 22; indeterminacy of, 146, 150, 156, 157–61; instability of, 99–101, 126, 127–30; ontological neutrality of, 6–7, 49, 119, 121, 137, 150, 162–64;

171

Cultural objects (*cont.*)
　ontology of, 6–7, 9, 32–36, 101; and praxial constructionism, 145. *See also* Practice-independent objects; *specific topics*
Cultural practices: consensual definition of, 39, 164; as context for cultural objects-of-interpretation, 13–18, 32, 37, 119–20; definitions of, 38–39; historical constitution of, 1–2, 31, 34, 37; vs. noncultural practices, 3–4; violation of, 40–41. See also Practice-independent objects; Praxial ideality
Cultures: ethnocentrism, 107–15; imputational interpretation of, 87–91; and personal programs, 85–86

Davidson, Donald, 61–62, 111, 144–45
Decisiveness, 50, 102
Demands, 44–47, 72n.9, 148
Diversity, 60
Donougho, Martin, 23–24
Dworkin, Ronald, 46n.8, 72n.9

Encyclopaedia of Mathematics, The (Hazelwinkel), 105–6
Error elimination, 43
Ethnocentrism, 107–11; consequences of, 111–15
Expressionism, 35–36
Extra-score considerations, 20–22, 29, 31–32, 54

Face-vase figures, 67–70
Feminist interpretations, 74–77
Ferrater-Mora, José, 39, 40
Formalist interpretations, 70, 72
Foundationalism, 6

Geertz, Clifford, 91, 107, 112–14
Ginastera, Alberto, 23
Gingold, Josef, 17
Global constructionism, 132–33
Goldstein, Leon, 131–33, 136–37, 138, 143, 144, 162, 163
Goodman, Nelson, 126, 140, 141
Graetz, H. R., 72–73, 74, 76, 77
Grossman, Morris, 33–34, 36, 148n.3, 149
Guilt cultures, 86, 89–90, 91

Hampshire, Stuart, 66, 148
Head Transformation (Samaras), 123, 124–25

Hirsch, E. D., 2, 48, 63, 77, 78, 79, 127–30
Historical interpretation, 131–45; Carr's theory, 138–40; multiplism in, 141–42; ontology in, 131–38, 141, 142–43; praxial constructionism in, 131, 140, 141, 142–45
Historicism, 5
Hodge, Joanna, 153
Hogwood, Christopher, 21
Hoy, David, 41
Human sciences, 5–6, 79–80

Ideally admissible interpretations, 8; arguments for, 22–26; constraints on range of, 49–53, 69–70, 94, 96; and error elimination, 43; as functions of cultural practices, 38, 39, 40; gradual distinctions, 28, 54; and intentions of creator, 23–24, 47–49, 50–51, 63, 79; of middle-sized objects, 157–58; multiplicity of, 32, 164; and nonconverging interpretations, 62–65; and performance, 17–18, 19–20n.8; and postulated creator, 24–25, 48–49, 50; and practice-independent objects, 36; and rational preferability, 28, 50; and reconstructability of creator's project, 25, 50–53; and self-understanding, 85; and unicity, 122. *See also* Pluralizing strategy; Singularism
Imputational interpretation, 6, 66–92; and anarchism, 96–97; circularity in, 98; and commonality, 121; constraints on, 69–70, 94, 96–97, 98; definition of, 67, 91–92, 93–94; of face-vase figures, 67–70; and historical developments, 95–96; and instability, 99–101; and ontology, 147; of other cultures, 87–91; and puzzle-solving vs. gratuitous interpretation, 98–99; in self-understanding, 79–87; and singularism, 97–98; of Van Gogh, 70–77; of Wordsworth, 77–79
Incommensurability, 30, 44, 50, 87–88, 90, 105–7
Inconclusivity. *See* Conclusivity
Indeterminacy, 128–30, 146–47, 150, 153–55; and practice-independent objects, 146–47, 157–61
Instability, 99–101, 126, 127–30
Intentionalism, 2, 48, 120n.2

INDEX

Intentions of creator, 23–24, 47–49, 50–51, 63, 79
Interpretation: admissible vs. inadmissible, 20–22, 53–54, 59–60, 165–66; aims of, 59–60; comparisons of, 2, 6; competition between, 97–98, 102, 122–23, 155, 156; critical, 18n.6; and description, 123, 126–27; distinction from cultural objects-of-interpretation, 98; extra-score considerations, 20–22, 29, 31–32, 54; formalist, 70, 72; infinite, 94–95, 96; of interpretation, 165; Marxist-feminist, 74–77, 104; nonconverging, 62–65; and performance, 18–19; psychological, 72–74, 104; puzzle-solving vs. gratuitous, 98–99. *See also* Ideally admissible interpretations; Imputational interpretation; *specific topics*
Interpretive anarchy, 49–53

Jakobson, Roman, 80
Jarvie, Ian, 43
Justification, 102, 104–5

Kandinsky, Wassily, 80
Kant, Immanuel, 120n.2, 165
Kiefer, Anselm, 63
Kuhn, Thomas, 5–6, 106

Language, 44–45, 107–11, 127–28, 153–55
Legal interpretation, 46n.8, 47
Leighton-Smith, Lawrence, 19
Levinson, Jerrold, 18n.6
Levi-Strauss, Claude, 148
Lubin, Albert, 73–74, 76, 77
Luo culture, 89–91, 167–69

MacIntyre, Alasdair, 62
Magee, Bryan, 14, 15–16
Mahler, Gustav, 55–56
Malevich, Casimir, 80
Margolis, Joseph, 48, 62–64, 67, 99–101, 120n.2, 122, 126, 129, 147n.1
Marxist-feminist interpretations, 74–77, 104
Mead, Margaret, 89–90
Mengelberg, Willem, 31, 40
Middle-sized objects, 5, 7, 120, 148, 157–58, 166
Milstein, Nathan, 14, 18
Mohanty, Jitendra, 109

Mothersill, Mary, 20n.8
Multiplism: and aims of interpretation, 59–60; and anarchy, 2, 49–53, 130; vs. critical pluralism, 41–42; definition of, 2, 27–28, 44; and ethnocentrism, 114; and extra-score considerations, 20–22, 29, 31–32, 54; in historical interpretation, 141–42; and imputational interpretation, 66–67, 93, 101; and incommensurability of standards, 30, 44; and language, 44–45; and natural sciences, 43; and ontology, 147, 162–64; plausibility of, 2–3; and postulated creator, 25; program of, 28–32; and rational preferability, 28–29, 50; as relativism, 60–62; and standards, 22, 29–30, 44, 54, 101. *See also specific topics*
Musical scores: admissible vs. inadmissible interpretations of, 20–22; counters to multiplism, 22–26; incompleteness of, 13–18, 22; multiplist program, 28–32
Muti, Riccardo, 15, 21, 28, 51–54, 103, 104, 147

Naive realism, 7
Natural sciences, 4–6, 42–43
Nehamas, Alexander, 2, 41, 149
Newsom, John, 18n.7
Newton, Isaac, 5
Nonconverging interpretations, 62–65
Noncultural practices, 3–4, 166
Norrington, Roger, 51–53
Novitz, David, 98–101, 126, 130, 151–52, 155
Nowell-Smith, Patrick, 2, 132, 134–37, 143, 148–50, 163

Objective music, 35
Objects-of-interpretation. *See* Cultural objects-of-interpretation
Occlusive fallacy, 151–52
Oistrakh, David, 14, 18
Ontological indeterminacy, 7
Ontological realism and constructionism: in historical interpretation, 131–38, 141, 142–43; and indeterminacy, 146–47, 159–61; and middle-sized objects, 5, 148; neutrality of objects-of-interpretation, 6–7, 49, 119, 121, 137, 150, 162–64; peacemeal vs. global, 148–49; and practice-independent objects, 32–33, 36, 101, 123, 126–27,

Ontological realism (*cont.*) 150–51; and singularism, 6, 32–36, 119, 162
Oxford English Dictionary, 128

Pan-intentionalism, 120n.2
Performance, 18–19, 33–34. *See also* Interpretation
Personal programs, 80–87, 113
Platonic entities, 7, 33, 36, 120
Pluralizing strategy, 31, 40, 41–42, 55–56, 57–60; and imputational interpretation, 74, 77, 79, 85; and unicity, 122, 156–57
Pollock, Griselda, 74–77
Popper, Karl, 2, 33, 35–36, 43, 81, 104–5, 120, 133, 148, 149, 151n.5, 162
Postulationism, 2
Potato Eaters (Van Gogh), 70–77, 123
Practice-independent objects, 7, 119, 120, 149; and constraints, 155–57; in historical interpretation, 136, 144–45; idea of, 150–53; and indeterminacy, 146–47, 157–61; and ontology, 32–33, 36, 101, 123, 126–27, 150–51
Pragmatism, 142–45
Praxial constructionism, 121, 126–27; in historical interpretation, 131, 137, 140–45; and indeterminacy, 160–61
Praxial ideality, 4, 7, 9, 39–41, 98. *See also* Cultural practices; Practice-independent objects; Praxial constructionism
Previn, André, 104
Psychological interpretations, 72–74, 104
Psychotherapy, 86
Putnam, Hilary, 66

Rational preferability, 28–29, 50
Realism. *See* Ontological realism and constructionism
Reconstructability of creator's project, 25, 50–53
Relativism, 60–62
Representation, 148
Rescher, Nicholas, 148
Rorty, Richard, 107, 111, 112–14
Rosen, Charles, 26

Salience, 68, 70, 74, 76–77, 123
Samaras, Lucas, 123, 124–25
Scale-tipping strategy, 45–47
Schafer, Roy, 86
Science. *See* Human sciences; Natural sciences
Scruton, Roger, 37
Self-understanding, 79–87, 91, 114, 121–22
Semantic autonomy, 130
Shame cultures, 86, 89–91
Singularism, 1; and conclusivity, 42; vs. critical monism, 41–42; definition of, 2, 27, 42; and imputational interpretation, 97–98; and interpretation of interpretation, 165; and noncultural practices, 166; and ontology, 6, 32–36, 119, 162; and philosophy of science, 42–43; and standards, 102; and strengthened demands, 44–47, 72n.9, 148; as universalist, 4. *See also* Ideally admissible interpretations; Pluralizing strategy; *specific topics*
"Slumber Did My Spirit Seal, A" (Wordsworth), 77–79
Spence, Donald, 86
Standards, 22, 29–30; and cultures, 90; incommensurability of, 30, 44, 50, 105–7; and intentions of creator, 47–49; local, 103; and nonconverging interpretations, 64–65; and ontological neutrality, 163–64; and relativism, 61; and self-understanding, 83, 84; and strengthened demands, 46, 72n.9. *See also* Conclusivity; Ideally admissible interpretations
Stokowski, Leopold, 31, 40, 56, 122
Strauss, Johann, 20
Structuralism, 148
Subjective music, 35

Taylor, Charles, 5, 6, 79–80, 87–88, 107–9
Tempo, 15–16
Toscanini, Arturo, 14, 15
Translatability, 62, 109–10
Tree, Michael, 19
Truth/falsity, 165–66

Unicity, 120–23, 156–57, 163–64
Universalism, 4

Values, 63–64
Van Gogh, Vincent, 70–77, 123

Wagner, Richard, 16, 35
Walter, Bruno, 14

Weitz, Morris, 72
Wittgenstein, Ludwig, 38n.1, 63, 72, 122
Wolterstorff, Nicholas, 33, 34, 36, 148n.3, 149
Wordsworth, William, 77–79

Zemach, E. M., 148, 157, 158–60, 163

Library of Congress Cataloging-in-Publication Data
Krausz, Michael.
Rightness and reasons : interpretation in cultural practices /
   Michael Krausz.
       p.   cm.
   Includes bibliographical references and index.
   ISBN 0-8014-2846-7 (alk. paper)
   1. Hermeneutics.   2. Aesthetics.   3. Ontology.   I. Title.
BD241.K74 1993
121'.68—dc20   93-12627